Thomas Jefferson:

From Shadwell To Poplar Forest

Janet Shaffer

Alexander Books
Alexander, North Carolina

An **Alexander Books** Publication

Publisher: Ralph Roberts
Editor: Philip Hawkins and Pat Roberts
Cover Design: Philip Hawkins
Interior Design and Electronic Page Assembly: **WorldComm®**

10 9 8 7 6 5 4 3 2 1

ISBN 1-57090-224-0

Alexander Books-a division of *Creativity, Inc.*-is a full-service publisher located at 65 Macedonia Road, Alexander NC 28701. Phone 1-828-252-9515, Fax 1-828-255-8719. For orders only: 1-800-472-0438. Visa and MasterCard accepted.

This book is also available on the Internet at **abooks.com.** Set your web browser to **http://abooks.com** and enjoy the many fine values available there.

Contents

Dedication

Dedicated to the Board of Directors, past and present, members of the staff, and to all the volunteers who make the restoration of Thomas Jefferson's Poplar Forest possible.

Acknowledgements

My sincere gratitude goes to Al Chambers for his encouragement and the use of his book as an invaluable reference, for his reading of early chapters of this book, and his encouragement in finding a publisher. I am equally indebted to other authorities for their knowledge of Poplar Forest and Thomas Jefferson within the framework of American history. If I have neglected to include anyone who deserves my thanks, please forgive me.

Foremost among these are the staff members at Poplar Forest who took the time to review and offer suggestions for the accuracy and overall direction of the manuscript during its various rewrites and revisions.

They are: Dianne M. Kinney, Manager of Visitor Services, for her special assistance throughout the manuscript preparation; Travis C. McDonald Jr., Director of Architectural Restoration, for his expertise; and Dr. Barbara Heath, Director of Archaeology and Landscapes, for her consultations with me over the years in regard to archeology. I am also grateful to Suzan Bryan, Manager, Poplar Forest Museum Shop; and Karen Sherbin, Director of Marketing and Public Relations; Octavia Starbuck, Director of Interpretation/Education; and Jackie Almond, Director of Information Technology. Thanks also to Sheryl Kingery, former Director of Interpretation. Special appreciation goes to Bill Barker, Interpreter of Thomas Jefferson at historic Colonial Williamsburg, for his enthusiasm and support.

I am also indebted to the competent professional people not associated with Poplar Forest who have read, edited, or evaluated the manuscript and offered helpful insights. Among these I would like to express my special appreciation to Dr. Wayne H. Wiley,

Professor of History at Central Virginia Community College, Lynchburg, Virginia, for his approval of the project and for his help and guidance. I would also like to thank Dr. John P. D'Entremont, Professor of History at Randolph-Macon Woman's College, Lynchburg, who double-checked the facts and content relating to American history and offered astute insights.

Not to be forgotten is Elizabeth Rosser Boiardi (Mrs. Daniele), Director of the American International School in Genoa, Italy, who, during her brief holidays to the U.S. from Genoa, helped organize my Poplar Forest computer files and offered tips on other computer problems relating to the preparation of the manuscript.

I also appreciate the assistance of several Poplar Forest docents who assisted in editing and were generally helpful. They are: tour docent volunteer, Gail Pond, who also serves as volunteer researcher and collections manager for Poplar Forest and offered invaluable help in multiple ways in the preparation of the manuscript. I also thank Dr. Marilyn Fisher, then-Division Chair for Humanities and Social Sciences, Central Virginia Community College, for editing and consultation, and Carol Patterson, a volunteer in the Museum Shop.

My heart was warmed by the graciousness of others in the Lynchburg community and area who gave support, encouraging reviews, or other assistance in the preparation of the chapters. I am especially grateful to Craig Shaffer, Director of Marketing & Communications at Progress Printing, for his help and support, and to the other members of my family. I want to thank two special friends, Sally Roseveare of Moneta and Wanda Garner of Lynchburg, who advised and supported me throughout the project. Others who helped are: Holly Frazier, then a history teacher at Heritage High School, and Lewis Averett, Coordinator of Public Services, Jones Memorial Library. I also want to recognize Caroline Matherly, former elementary school teacher and librarian in the Bedford Public Library, and Amanda

Michelle Shober, then a student at E.C.Glass High School and Mary Rogers, then-branch manager of Timbrook Library in Campbell County.

I would not want to end this list of acknowledgments without thanking Dorsey Bodeman, the first Interpretation Coordinator at Poplar Forest. Prior to launching her volunteer recruits on tours to show the house to visitors, she acquainted all of us with the history of the plantation, rehearsed sample tours and suggested successful strategies for handling groups. Overall, Bodeman set high standards for each volunteer whether serving as docents, or working in some other capacity.

Jefferson's private retreat at Poplar Forest.

From the Collections of Thomas Jefferson's Poplar Forest. Photograph by Travis McDonald.

Jefferson's formal home, Monticello, near Charlottesville, Virginia.

Courtesy of Monticello, Thomas Jefferson Foundation, Inc.

Preface

I have written this easy-read book, *Thomas Jefferson: From Shadwell to Poplar Forest,* for the countless admirers of Thomas Jefferson in the general reading public who may want to learn more about this extraordinary man and about Poplar Forest, the plantation villa he designed and built as a retreat in Bedford County, Virginia. In that sense, it is an abbreviated dual biography of one of our nation's greatest leaders–and of the beloved retreat that became an integral part of his personal history.

As background for the story of its construction, I have interwoven highlights of Jefferson's private life, along with his achievements in public office, and as writer, thinker, builder, philosopher, scientist and his other pursuits.

It was at Poplar Forest that as a mature architect, he built an octagonal house of classical design where he found solitude and the leisure to carry on his favorite pursuits–to think, to study, and to read from some of his favorite books. Among these were the classics in the original Greek and Latin, history, British and Italian poets, Shakespeare and others he kept in his private collection at his retreat.

After Jefferson retired from holding government office, in 1809, he reveled in his new role as private citizen and enjoyed the leisure to visit his Bedford County retreat three or more times a year and while there, oversaw its on-going construction and the farming operations. The man and his cherished "second home" cannot be separated.

My introduction to Thomas Jefferson and Poplar Forest began in 1984 when I first agreed to serve as a volunteer house tour guide (or docent) at the then-vacant house that was slated for restoration. I re-volunteered each year thereafter. The story of the building of the retreat, its history, and of Jefferson himself so fired my imagination that I wanted to learn more and to share the fascinating story with visitors.

Another important motivation for writing this dual biography was my discovery that in contrast to the many books and an abundance of other published material on Monticello, only one book (that had been fully approved and endorsed by the Corporation), had been written about Poplar Forest up until that time. An authority on Jefferson and his retreat house, S. Allen Chambers, Jr., wrote and published an outstanding scholarly volume in 1993 entitled *Poplar Forest and Thomas Jefferson*. Chambers' comprehensive research and the overall excellence of his book helped pave the way for this more simplified and abbreviated account.

A second book on Poplar Forest, written and researched by Joan L. Horn, entitled *Thomas Jefferson's Poplar Forest* (subtitled: *A Private Place),* was published in 2002. It is a guidebook compilation of facts about Jefferson's retreat that brings the restoration and archeology research up-to-date. The copyright is held by The Corporation for Thomas Jefferson's Poplar Forest.

Through the years, Poplar Forest volunteers have been encouraged to read and digest reams of printed material dealing with Jefferson as the designer and architect of his rural retreat. As part of our "education" we also learned much about the man himself— his private life, political career, and his impressive architectural achievements. In addition, we became acquainted with Jefferson's life at Poplar Forest, as slave owner, as father and grandfather, as neighbor, as farmer/agronomist, as self-taught architect, in short as a brilliant multi-talented man of many facets.

Professional staff members continue to conduct annual refresher workshops and training sessions for all volunteers. The insistence on excellence, continued learning, and the perfecting of skills helps assure high levels of interpretation of Jefferson's property to the flood of visitors who find their way to his retreat to learn about the building of Poplar Forest.

In 1821 Jefferson described his retreat in a letter to William Short, his former secretary in France, friend and protégé: *I have an excellent house there, am comfortably fixed and attended, have a few good neighbors, and pass my time there in tranquility and retirement much adapted to my age and indolence.*

Author Janet Shaffer mingles with Thomas Jefferson at a reception held at Jefferson's retreat, Poplar Forest. Jefferson is interpreted by Bill Barker of historic Colonial Williamsburg.

Photograph by Joe Swope.

The Rudolph Evans' bronze sculpture of Jefferson presides over the Jefferson Memorial in Washington, D.C. The 19-foot high statue weighs 10,000 pounds.

Photograph by the author.

Introduction

In 1981, the future of Thomas Jefferson's Poplar Forest Retreat in Bedford County, Virginia was uncertain. The previous summer Dr. James A. Johnson, a Jefferson admirer and a physician from High Point, North Carolina, had bought the then-vacant house. He hoped to keep the estate safe from development until it could be bought by a historical organization or foundation and restored to its former beauty.

Local historical groups knew that despite Dr. Johnson's intervention, Jefferson's former estate was still threatened. Members of one of these groups joined forces to mobilize a fund drive to purchase the house, outbuildings, and remaining Jefferson land. Despite their best efforts they failed to raise enough money.

Fortunately, a new group, later called the Corporation for Thomas Jefferson's Poplar Forest, came to the rescue, and on December 18, 1983, signed a contract to purchase the main house and the remaining 50 acres in one parcel as well as an additional parcel containing 255 acres for a combined price of $1,800,000. The deed was recorded at the Bedford County Courthouse. The disparity in land values over the decades is evident in a statement made by Jefferson in 1814. He wrote that the house was worth $10,000. Ironically, two years after his death in 1826, his grandson, Francis Eppes, sold the house and just over 1,000 acres of land, for $4,925 to a neighbor, William Cobbs.

Since 1983, the non-profit Corporation has purchased additional land bringing the total to 570 acres of Jefferson's original 4,819-acre plantation tract. Land acquisitions included the grounds directly adjacent to the main house: the golf course and swim/tennis club, the former Camp Ruthers property and land where one of Jefferson's tobacco-drying barns once stood.

From the beginning, the goal of the Corporation has been to preserve and restore Poplar Forest for future generations and open it to the public. Twenty years have passed since that time. The transformation has been extraordinary, the result of wise planning and strong leadership.

Lynn Beebe, Executive Director of the Corporation for Thomas Jefferson's Poplar Forest comments, "Poplar Forest was an important part of Jefferson's life: a private retreat, situated far from the public scrutiny and demands on his time of which he had grown so weary. It was his most personal architectural creation and landscape, a place where he came to find rest and leisure, to rekindle his creativity, and to enjoy private family time."

It was an enormous undertaking, especially considering that a fire in 1845 had severely damaged the dwelling. Even so, the staff, headed by Beebe, and the Board of Directors, determined to restore the house and grounds with as high a degree of accuracy as possible, combining today's state-of-the-art research expertise with highly skilled craftsmen knowledgeable in the art of historic restoration and the use of traditional tools from Jefferson's era.

"It's an uncanny thing reliving Jefferson's process," says Travis McDonald, Poplar Forest's Director of Architectural Restoration. "There is no way we would have had the same insights if we didn't go through the same methods and use the same materials." In 1989, stabilization of the house marked the first phase of the renewal process. The second phases, conservation work combined with the investigative and research stages began in 1990 and continued throughout 1992, preceding the actual restoration.

Gradually, the mysteries of Jefferson's retreat began to unravel. Besides sleuthing and exploring the physical remains of the property, research scholars were assigned to locate and examine his journals, letters, memorandum books, and other Jeffersonian papers. These were stored at university libraries, various archives, and at other locations across the country; the search demanded time, travel, skill, and intense research efforts

Crowds gather to hear the Declaration of Independence read every July 4 at Jefferson's retreat, Poplar Forest. The readings took place even while the home's exterior underwent restoration; exterior restoration was completed in 1998.

Photograph by the author.

An architectural conservator, a team of architects and an architectural advisory panel led by Travis McDonald, met to discuss the art of conserving and restoring the architecture of historic buildings.

The restoration at Poplar Forest is being accomplished using a unique approach focusing on the building methods that Jefferson's craftsmen used when the retreat home was originally built. Restoring the historic house required architects and craftsmen with specialized skills familiar with traditional building techniques and materials.

Archaeologists, currently led by Dr. Barbara Heath, Director of Archaeology & Landscapes, joined in the exploration and the continuing search for history. Their ongoing goal was, and is, to dig for buried clues to the past, and continue to discover more about Jefferson, his family members, and the community of enslaved workers who lived at Poplar Forest at that time.

Heath points to the vital and versatile roles of the slave plantation community in the construction of Jefferson's octagonal house.
"After 1805, when the construction of Jefferson's octagonal house
began," she comments, "Jerry, Phil Hubbard, and Hemings worked
with hired artisans in brick making, masonry and carpentry.
Through excavation and massive earthmoving, Phil worked to
create the sunken south lawn and ornamental mounds. Jame
Hubbard's grandson, Nace, tended Jefferson's vegetable garden,
nursery, and landscape pleasure grounds."

The creation of a foundation to insure future preservation of
the house was achieved with the installation of footings. Completed brickwork, restoration of Jefferson's original window and
door openings and repairs to the original columns on the north
and south porticos produced spectacular results.

Four elongated octagonal rooms surround the dining room.
Workmen raised the walls in the central room to the original
twenty-foot cubic dimension and restored the over-sixteen-foot
skylight and the dining room's "terras" (or flat) roof. Additional
interior restoration, such as the installation of tongue-and-grooved
white oak floors throughout the house was completed. More concentrated work on the interior lies ahead.

The restoration of exterior architectural elements included
a balustrade, a Chinese railing and cornice. By the end of 1993,
for the first time since the disastrous fire in 1845, Poplar Forest's
completed exterior looked just as Thomas Jefferson had designed it.

With the restoration of the east and west octagonal privies
(necessaries) in 2002, new and exciting interior restoration began with the plastering of interior walls in 2003. The finished
reconstruction of Jefferson's wing of dependencies (or service
rooms), originally built by enslaved carpenters in 1814, is slated
for 2006.

The retreat house and grounds opened to the public in 1986.
Despite inconveniences, such as scaffolding around much of the
buildings and the sound of hammers and other sound effects, guests

on the property could see craftsmen working on an historic house and feel part of the actual restoration.

Visitors from across America and from foreign countries have been welcomed to Jefferson's "second home" throughout the preservation and restoration stages. In 2002, approximately 28,000 people visited the retreat. Over 100 volunteers serve as house tour guides, as assistants in the Poplar Forest Museum Shop, in the archaeology lab or in other capacities.

One of the most important tasks is helping in the educational program, conducting special tours of the house and grounds for busloads of school children, and most recently, assisting in the fascinating Hands-on-History learning area. This innovation is designed to give students the opportunity to experience various aspects of daily life at Poplar Forest during Thomas Jefferson's time. Led by a staff Hands-on-History Leader, students are given the opportunity to interact with docents, participate in hands-on-activities, such as traditional brick making and writing with a quill pen, and learn critical thinking skills to interpret, analyze and evaluate history.

The rejuvenation of Jefferson's architectural gem has been a time of learning and fitting together the pieces of a giant puzzle. During the years that have elapsed since the beginning of its conservation and restoration, milestones have been reached in bringing the original goal closer to reality. The project continues to be a work in progress.

Funding from grants and gifts will hasten the projected restoration of Thomas Jefferson's Poplar Forest retreat.

A Brief Timeline of the Life of Thomas Jefferson

1743   Jefferson born at Shadwell in Virginia.

1760   Jefferson enters the College of William and Mary.

1772   Jefferson marries Martha Wayles Skelton.

1773   Jefferson visits Poplar Forest for the first time to view the 4,819-acre plantation following the death of his father-in-law.

1776   Jefferson writes the Declaration of Independence.

1781   Jefferson and his family escape to Poplar Forest to avoid capture by the British during the American Revolution.

1781   Jefferson writes parts of his book *Notes on the State of Virginia.*

1801   Jefferson is elected President of the United States.

1806   Construction begins on Jefferson's house at Poplar Forest

1809   Jefferson begins to make regular trips to Poplar Forest, three to four times a year.

1816   Jefferson's granddaughters begin their many visits to Poplar Forest.

1819   Jefferson establishes the University of Virginia.

1826   Jefferson dies on July 4th

CHAPTER 1

YOUNG FRONTIERSMAN

By going to the College I shall get a more universal Acquaintance, which may hereafter be serviceable to me; and I suppose I can pursue my Studies in the Greek and Latin as well there as here, and likewise learn something of the Mathematics.

Thomas Jefferson, to John Harvie, one of his guardians, 1760

Thomas Jefferson, who played an important role in the destiny of his country, was born April 13, 1743, in a frontier settlement nestled below a gap in the Southwest Mountains in the colony of Virginia. His father Peter had built a small two-story wooden house, in view of the Blue Ridge Mountains, that he named Shadwell after a parish in London where, twenty-three years before, his wife, Jane Randolph, had been christened.

Peter Jefferson was one of the first pioneers to homestead in a newly opened area called Albemarle County, which in 1744 was formed from the counties of Goochland and Louisa. Granted rights to ownership of one thousand acres along the Rivanna River, he later bought another four hundred. With hard work, he carved a small plantation from the wilderness. Peter and Jane Jefferson were already the parents of two daughters. Thomas was the third child, the first boy born into the household.

Young Thomas' earliest memories were not of Shadwell, however, but of Tuckahoe, a plantation in Goochland County on the James River not far from Richmond, where he spent the early years of his boyhood. At age two or three, Thomas moved with the Jefferson family to Tuckahoe after the premature death of a family friend, Colonel William Randolph. Before his death the Colonel had made a will with an unusual request. He had asked Peter Jefferson, his "dear and loving friend," to serve as manager and custodian of Tuckahoe and to help oversee the rearing of his three motherless children. Feeling obliged to honor the colonel's request, the Jeffersons lived for approximately six years in the Randolph house. At age five, Thomas attended a small private school on the property, probably with his older sisters and the three Randolph orphans.

Finally, in 1752, when the Randolph children were older and no longer needed his close care and guardianship, Peter decided that the time had come to return to Shadwell with his family. Thomas, by then nine years old, had sandy-red hair, a sprinkle of freckles across his thin cheeks, and hazel-tinted eyes. Gangly-limbed and tall for his age, some of his friends are said to have called him "Long Tom."

A self-taught frontiersman, Peter Jefferson wanted Thomas to have a good classical education and enrolled him in a small Latin boarding school taught by the Reverend William Douglas. The log school was close enough to Shadwell to allow Thomas to ride his horse back and forth on weekends and holidays. He made friends with the other boys and besides completing his schoolwork, read many of the books in the clergyman's library.

During long summers at home, Thomas very likely acquired a practical education not found in books. An unusually studious boy, he also learned from reading and from listening to and watching the slaves work at their various tasks. Growing up on a farm, he would also have learned the basics of gardening and raising tobacco, the main money crop of most plantation owners of the day, as well as the names of fruits and vegetables. In addition, he may have gained some knowledge of a variety of other farm activities and crafts. These would have included shoeing horses and the care and breeding of all kinds of livestock and a basic knowledge of farming.

At a young age, Thomas knew how to shoot a gun, track game, hunt and paddle a canoe. One day, his father gave him a gun and sent him into the woods alone, probably hoping to teach his son self-reliance. As the family account goes, at first the young huntsman could find no game to shoot, but finally, he discovered an unharmed wild turkey caught in a box trap, removed it, tied the fowl to a tree with his garter, shot it, and carried it home in triumph.

Throughout the frontier area, Peter Jefferson was known for his endurance and physical prowess. According to tales about his strength, he could lift wooden storage barrels called hogsheads and toss them onto a wagon as though they were goose-down pillows. Each barrel weighed hundreds of pounds.

It is said that on another occasion, his father looped a rope around an old shed, took a deep breath, and pulled it to the ground. Three men standing by watched in amazement as he performed the exploit. They had pushed with their combined strengths but failed to push the shed down.

Like others, Thomas must have marveled at such feats of strength but he also admired his father for other reasons. Peter Jefferson had had no formal schooling as a child (teachers and schools were scarce in those early frontier days) but alert and quick of mind, he knew how to produce crops and had mastered a variety of skills and practical crafts. In 1754, when Thomas was eleven, his father was elected to the Virginia General Assembly to represent Albemarle County in the House of Burgesses, an important ruling body in colonial government.

Perhaps using drafting and surveying instruments were the most important of Peter's various skills, together with his ability to make maps. Young Thomas must have been impressed when his father and Joshua Fry, a former teacher of mathematics at the College of William and Mary in Williamsburg, were commissioned to locate and mark the boundary lines between Virginia and North Carolina. As partners they completed their assignment successfully, but while doing so suffered many hardships and perils. By 1751, they had finished making their now-famous map of Virginia. The Fry-Jefferson map, entitled *A Map of the Inhabited Part of Virginia,* was first published in London in 1754, or early 1755, and was regarded as one of the best maps of its time.

As Thomas grew older he, too, learned to work with surveying instruments. He taught himself to observe carefully and to remember landmarks such as rocks, trees and other vegetation. Curious since childhood, he was a boy who liked to discover the source of creeks and streams and to explore nature.

This same curiosity led Thomas as an adult to be fascinated with architecture, archaeology, meteorology, mechanical devices, and other areas of science. Throughout his life he spent time and energy learning more about each one and making them an important part of his private world.

During the summer of 1757, when Thomas was fourteen, his father became seriously ill. Through the month of June, Peter's friend and physician Doctor Thomas Walker came often to treat his sick patient and continued to do so through July and part of August. However, his medical remedies and efforts were in vain. Only fifty years of age, Peter died on August 17, leaving his family distraught. By then there were eight children. Besides the oldest, Jane, there were Mary, Thomas, Elizabeth, Martha, Lucy, and the twins Anna and Thomas' only brother, Randolph. Two other baby boys born to Jane Randolph Jefferson at Tuckahoe had not survived.

Thomas knew that no one could ever take the place of his beloved father. He was grief-stricken and lonely without him for a long time afterwards. Sometimes, to console himself, he wandered off alone into the mountains where he had often walked with his father. One mountain in particular he had loved since boyhood and thought of as his own. He even dreamed of someday building himself a house there at its summit.

Peter Jefferson had willed Thomas his choice of two tracts of land when he reached the age of twenty-one. One was the Rivanna River property, and the other was on the Fluvanna (which later became known as the James River). His father also left him a sufficient sum of money to pay for a classical education as well as the collection of books in his small library, his surveying instruments and various other personal belongings.

Before his death, Peter Jefferson had named two executors of his estate to whom Thomas sometimes went for advice. They both agreed that he should continue his schooling. Their choice was a school for boys operated and taught by the Reverend James Maury, an Anglican minister and an exceptional classical scholar. His log school was approximately fourteen miles from Shadwell. Once again Thomas could board away from home but spend time with his family when the school was closed. He was a diligent student because he liked to learn—whether it was mathematics, classical studies, languages, physics, history, grammar, literature, or geography.

The executors of Peter Jefferson's will apparently recognized the importance of a well-rounded education for a young Virginia gentleman. According to family records Thomas took lessons on the violin (which he enjoyed) and in his spare time, along with his sisters, learned to dance.

Besides offering his pupils a superior education in the classical languages, Greek and Latin, and other subjects, the Reverend James Maury extended his instruction to the outdoors. He took the boys hiking and riding and on explorations through mountains, fields, and forests. When classes were over for the day, Thomas and his best friend, Dabney Carr, tracked wild game to their dens and memorized the names of trees and plants (flora) and many of the birds and animals (fauna) in nature. During vacations from school, he and Jane, his favorite sister, took long walks in the woodlands near Shadwell to enjoy the beauty of the outdoors.

After approximately two years at the Maury school, Thomas wrote a letter about his future to one of the executors his father had appointed. He wrote that he was ready and eager to continue his education at the College of William and Mary in Williamsburg, Virginia. In the letter he said that he could continue his study of the classics at the college, learn something of mathematics, and gain "a more universal acquaintance" there.

At age seventeen, when Thomas rode to Williamsburg in the spring of 1760 to begin his new life, he probably felt shy and a little unsure of himself, wondering if he would be able to keep up with his studies and if his clothes were sufficiently stylish so that the other boys would not tease him.

After Shadwell, the town of Williamsburg with its two hundred or more houses must have seemed huge and almost overwhelming to the young countryman. He soon discovered, however, that it was a lively, busy place where exciting things happened. Teams of horses pulled ornately decorated coaches along the roads made of sand and oyster shells. Handsomely dressed men and women occupied the coaches or paraded up and down Duke of Gloucester Street. Tradesmen, shopkeepers and craftspeople displayed their wares to passersby. Political bigwigs, plantation owners and ordinary citizens of the town frequented the bustling taverns to dine on venison, stews, and such hearty fare. They also gathered to talk and to drink French wines, punch, rum, or brandy.

As a young student, Thomas could not afford the price of food or drink at such establishments, but on rare occasions he ate supper at the Raleigh Tavern. With his friends, he went to horse races, cockfights, fiddling contests, and other enjoyable outdoor entertainment.

Something was always going on in the evenings. When he could afford the price of a ticket, Thomas attended the theater to watch troupes of traveling actors perform Shakespearean plays. He also accepted invitations to parties and fancy balls where he enjoyed the frivolity and danced the reels, minuets and other popular dances of the day.

Most mornings he was up early, and to the amazement (and probably the amusement) of his roommates, Thomas took his daily exercise by running at least two miles through the streets. Also each morning, heeding the advice his father had once given him, he soaked his feet in cold water to prevent colds.

It was predictable that with his quick, questioning mind and ability to master difficult subjects with ease, he would impress his teachers. He particularly impressed William Small, professor of natural philosophy. Professor Small also taught classes in physics, metaphysics and mathematics. As time went on, Thomas and his favorite teacher became friends. Before long, Small introduced the promising young student from Shadwell to two of his close friends. Both were men of importance, learning, and wisdom who were to influence Thomas' thinking–and his future direction.

One of these friends was George Wythe, a highly respected Williamsburg lawyer who would become his teacher in the study of law. The other was Governor Francis Fauquier, an economist with interests in physics and natural sciences who was a cultured mannerly man. Soon after meeting the young student, Fauquier invited Thomas, together with Small and Wythe to musical concerts at the Governor's Palace and to join their dinner groups.

On those occasions or seated at tavern tables, Jefferson, Small, Fauquier and Wythe often engaged in stimulating conversations on such topics as art, natural history, philosophy, political history, and law. Thomas later said that during his frequent visits to the palace with his new friends he had heard "more good sense, more rational and philosophical conversations" than at any other time in his life.

One of the unforgettable events that occurred during his student days at the College of William and Mary concerned a great Cherokee Indian chief, Ontassete who was also known as Ostenaco or Oconasta.

As some tribes had a habit of doing, the chief and a group of his followers, came to visit the colonial capital in the spring of 1762. The news quickly spread that Chief Ontassete had been invited to visit the King of England. According to the report, he was to make a farewell oration that night at a nearby Cherokee campsite before sailing the next day across the Atlantic Ocean.

Thomas was intrigued. That evening he visited the camp, and as the story goes, he heard Ontassete speak in a deep resonant voice as he prayed for a safe ocean crossing and for the prosperity and protection of the Cherokee people during his absence.

The weather was cool. The moon, big and round as a wheel, lightened the sky and sprayed gold on the scene below. Ontassete's followers, hunching close to their campfires, listened in solemn silence.

Thomas, too, listened silently, awe-struck. Years before, as a boy, he had met Ontassete when his father had invited the great chief and his followers to camp outside their Shadwell home and to visit with the Jefferson family as guests—and as equals.

His father's friendships with Indians deeply impressed him and probably helped inspire his lifelong fascination with Native Americans. Sometime during the 1770s, when Jefferson was still a young man, his interest in Indians led him to organize an archaeological expedition to a large Monocan Indian mound located north of Charlottesville, Virginia. Later, in 1787, in *Notes on the State of Virginia* (his only published book), he wrote his analysis and conclusions about the dig.

Jefferson directed the excavation, and oversaw the removal of a series of layers of soil, or *strata,* with great care. By doing so, he introduced the theory of stratification that is based on the principle that in time, soil accumulates in layers, with the oldest layer being buried deepest and the youngest layer on top. Each layer of soil contains objects dating to the time they were deposited. As archaeologists find and analyze these artifacts, they are able to determine the passage of time, study past human behavior and interpret history.

In his excavation of the burial site, Thomas Jefferson discovered and used some of the principles, aims, and methods on which the science of modern archaeology is based. Today, he is recognized as the first scientific archaeologist and he is sometimes called the "Father of American Archaeology."

Jefferson's fascination with and curiosity about North American Indian tribes increased rather than diminished over the years. He wanted to learn more about their populations, geographical locations, cultures, languages, dress, and native customs. Much later in his life, while serving as the President of the United States, he was able to do so. His interest in Indians led him to make decisions and influence legislation that greatly changed history and the future growth and development of America.

Native Americans were among the performers who brought their heritage to life when the nationally touring Corps of Discovery II came to Poplar Forest as part of the commemoration of the Lewis and Clark expedition's Bicentennial. Jefferson had directed the expedition to learn as much as possible about the western tribes.

From the Collections of Thomas Jefferson's Poplar Forest. Photograph by Karin Sherbin.

View of Monticello, a painting by Braddick c. 1825
Courtesy of Monticello, Thomas Jefferson Foundation, Inc.

CHAPTER 2

ENDINGS AND NEW BEGINNINGS

I have lately removed to the mountain from whence this is dated. I have here but one room, which like the cobler's serves me for parlour for kitchen and hall. I may add, for bed chamber and study too. My friends sometimes take a temperate dinner with me and then retire to look for beds elsewhere. I have hopes however of getting more elbow room this summer.

Stated in one of Jefferson's earliest known letters written from Monticello, to James Ogilvie, February 20, 1771.

After two years at the College of William and Mary, Jefferson decided to become a lawyer. At age nineteen, he felt ready to earn his own living. In 1762, there were no formal law schools, so for approximately five years he read legal books in Williamsburg under the guidance of his friend and advisor George Wythe who helped qualify his protégé to practice law.

Following his twenty-first birthday, Jefferson was eligible to receive the inheritance his father had written into his will. He knew he must choose between the Rivanna River tract and that of the

Fluvanna. For reasons of his own, he chose the Rivanna property perhaps because of the mountaintop that overlooked rolling hills and deep valleys where he had spent many hours reading and playing during his boyhood, and where he liked to dream about the future.

The Rivanna tract contained 2,000 acres, and with the addition of several other pieces of land, he inherited around 5,000 acres, twenty-two slaves, and the gristmill that he operated until a flood swept it away in 1771. His younger brother Randolph would, at age twenty-one, inherit the Fluvanna tract that was of nearly equal size.

During the early years of his law practice, Jefferson traveled frequently between Albemarle and Williamsburg where he apparently had an office and living quarters. Along the way, he sometimes stopped in towns and county seats to attend to legal business, and he helped his mother with the financial and agricultural affairs of Shadwell plantation that was legally hers for life.

At leisurely moments during these early years, he began the practice of jotting down bits and pieces of information in a ledger or journal. These brief notes were the beginning of his *Garden Book*. One day in March he wrote: *Purple hyacinth begins to bloom*. Later, he wrote that the blue flowers in the lowlands had finished blooming, and jotted down other botanical observations.

Thereafter and for the rest of his life, Jefferson recorded detailed information about *flowers, vegetables, fruits, and the wide variety of trees and plants which flourished in the* red clay soil of central Virginia.

Over the years, Jefferson took record keeping more and more seriously. In his *Garden Book* he continued to record what he planted, the location of vegetable beds, and crop production at harvest time. He also kept *Memorandum Books* in which he jotted down expenditures, law cases, and random facts about a variety of business-related subjects. In his *Farm Book* he made notations about seasonal activities, the outlay of expenses at his various plantations and other data. Always the scientist, in his *Weather Memorandum Book* he recorded such day-to-day occurrences as temperatures, wind direction and rainfall. He continued to write in most of his books, ledgers and journals until a few weeks before he died.

Soon after his twenty-fifth birthday in 1768, Jefferson decided not to delay an architectural project that had been on his mind for some time. He wanted to design and build a mountaintop house that overlooked the fields and valleys below. He gave orders to workmen to cut a road through the forest and clear and level an expanse of land at its summit. The next year they excavated a cellar as the foundation for a small one-room brick cottage where he planned to live until he could move into the main house he would build. Next, they dug a well, made bricks and completed other preparations to build the first structure on the property.

At first, Jefferson had considered calling his mountaintop home "The Hermitage," perhaps because a hermitage can be defined as a secluded place in a solitary location. Later, however, he chose the name Monticello, which translated from the Italian language means "little mountain."

The satisfaction of having a place of his own, no matter how small in the beginning, was especially timely considering the tragic fire at Shadwell plantation on February 1, 1770, that destroyed the house Peter Jefferson had built for his wife and children. Naturally, everyone in the family felt sad and heartsick over the loss of their home. That afternoon, Jefferson spent time at Shadwell with his family but later in the day went to Charlottesville on business. The flames had not harmed any member of the family, but Jefferson bemoaned the loss of most of his books, papers, the cherry-tree desk, bookcase, and other treasures he had inherited from his father. He was grateful that at least his violin had been spared and his *Garden Book* and other journals were safe in the cottage being built for him at Monticello. Though it may not have been completely finished, he moved into his new home the following November. The other members of his family stayed at Shadwell after the fire, living as best they could in the remaining buildings.

His new living quarters were conveniently close to his mother's land holdings in Albemarle she had asked him to help supervise. Even more important, as both the architect and builder of Monticello, he could oversee the ongoing construction of his house.

There were no schools of architecture in Virginia in Jefferson's day. He learned from observation and from books. It is thought that he had bought a second-hand book (his first) on architecture while he was still a student at William and Mary. The purchase marked the beginning of what would become an impressive collection on the subject.

In his early plans and drawings for Monticello, Jefferson was most influenced by British architects James Gibbs, Robert Morris, and William Kent, and even more so by the sixteenth century master architect Andrea Palladio, who had used models and rules dating back to Roman antiquity. The English architects had imitated some of Palladio's ideas, such as simplicity, serenity, and reserve. Jefferson came to value these and other architectural principles in designing and building both Monticello and, eventually, his Poplar Forest retreat in Bedford County. These were the only two houses he ever built for his own use.

A second influence affecting Jefferson's views on architecture was his classical education at William and Mary, which created a life-long intense interest and wide study of the ancient classical world. A third influence was the five years he later spent abroad as Minister to France. During his travels in France, Italy, and elsewhere, he admired much of the architecture, sculpture, painting and music. He was also impressed by many of the ancient and modern European buildings he saw, including the fashionable, intimate townhouses of the day, called hotels. He much admired the salon of the Casa Belgioioso in Milan, Italy, and while viewing the remains of Roman grandeur in Nimes, France, he was awed by the Maison Quaree, an ancient structure he sketched and remembered when making plans for the architecture of the Virginia State Capitol.

By 1770, Jefferson's career as a young lawyer was going well. Already he was recognized for his thoroughness, fairness and intelligence in dealing with people. The year before, he had been elected as a delegate from Albemarle County to the Virginia House of Burgesses, which was the ruling legislature for the colony. In the spring, he had taken the oath of office with almost one hundred other delegates in the Council chamber of the Capitol and was seated as a new member. He was twenty-six years old. It was the beginning of a long political career of patriotic service to his country.

The year 1770 was a momentous year for still another reason. After an earlier failed romance, he had made no serious effort to court young ladies until he met a beautiful twenty-one year-old widow, Martha Wayles Skelton. She was the daughter of John Wayles, a well-known lawyer and owner of a plantation estate called The Forest in Charles City County, not far from Williamsburg.

His visits to Martha's home increased. According to family accounts, Martha had an attractive figure, expressive hazel eyes, and dark auburn red hair. He also discovered that she was intelligent and charming, and an accomplished musician. As the love affair continued, the two spent many hours together playing duets–he on the violin or the cello, she at the pianoforte or on the harpsichord. They also attended plays and concerts, horse races, and other entertainment in or near Williamsburg.

They were married on New Year's Day, 1772, at The Forest. The family story goes that the young couple stayed two weeks at Martha's home before setting out for Monticello. On the way, they stopped at Tuckahoe where the bridegroom had lived during his early boyhood years, but once again they were delayed in reaching their destination, Monticello. A January blizzard unleashed its white fury and further travel by phaeton (carriage) became almost impossible. According to the story, they stopped at Blenheim, the home of family friends, where they left the phaeton and rode the remaining eight miles on horseback. When they finally reached Monticello after the long journey of more than a hundred miles, night had fallen and three feet of snow covered the ground.

At first, things must have looked dismal to the newly-weds. The servants had gone to bed and no cheerful fire blazed on the hearth. The bridegroom soon had a fire going, however, and in a surprise move, brought forth a half bottle of wine from behind a row of books on a shelf. The couple honeymooned in the groom's bachelor quarters and continued to live there until they could occupy his unfinished mansion house, Monticello. The construction work was well underway, but it would be years (if ever) before it would provide the domestic comforts to which the bride had been accustomed.

The first September after their marriage, they rejoiced over the birth of a daughter, Martha, whom they often called Patsy.

In the spring of 1773, Jefferson was saddened by the premature death from an unknown fever of his boyhood friend, Dabney Carr, not yet thirty, who had married Jefferson's sister, Martha. Forever afterward, he felt a brotherly concern and responsibility for helping her with her financial and legal affairs. He also tried to be a substitute father to her six children, and eventually, at his invitation, the Carr family came to live at Monticello.

That same spring, the death of John Wayles, Martha Jefferson's father, brought even more sorrow to the pair. When the Wayles' estate was settled, Martha inherited over 11,000 acres and 135 slaves. However, she and her husband discovered that John Wayles had also left unpaid debts behind that would become a financial burden to Jefferson for many years to come.

Included in Martha's share of her father's land holdings was a tract of nearly 5,000 acres called Poplar Forest in Bedford County, Virginia. Jefferson was curious about the property and decided to go there in September 1773, to look over the land. A slave, Jupiter, went along. In his *Memorandum Book*, Jefferson recorded paying "ferriage at Davies's ferry" and "Lynch's ferry" and payment for entertainment in the town of New London, just three miles from Poplar Forest.

Jefferson was not disappointed by what he found at the end of the three-day journey. The fertile tract of land was already a working

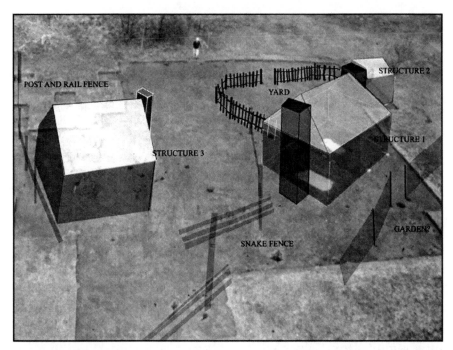

Up to ninety-four enslaved workers lived at Poplar Forest during Jefferson's time. Archaeologists have excavated two Jefferson-era slave quarter sites, enabling them to interpret what the slaves' housing and lives were like.

From the Collections of Thomas Jefferson's Poplar Forest. Illustration by Edmund Potter.

plantation with tobacco, wheat, and other crops under cultivation that showed promise of profitable harvests to boost his yearly income. He saw an assortment of farm outbuildings, log cabins used as slave quarters and a small overseer's cabin, but as far as is known, no manor house. There were lush meadows for grazing livestock and streams for irrigation running through the property.

In the distance, the new landowner also saw the Blue Ridge Mountains rimming the fields and abundant forests. In 1820, Jefferson was to list in his *Garden Book* the names of the various mountains visible from Poplar Forest. Among these were No Business, Fleming's Mountain, and a vista of Tobacco Row Mountain.

One of the recordings Jefferson made in his *Farm Book* at the time of his first visit to Poplar Forest in 1773 dealt with the farm activities and the names of slaves. Among these he mentioned

"Billy boy," the blacksmith, family groups such as Will and Judy and their children, Jemmy and York, and Tom Shackleford and Amy. Of the 27 slaves he listed in Bedford by the end of 1774, many of the adults, whom he called "labourers in the ground," worked in the tobacco fields.

It is not definitely known when the property was first called Poplar Forest, but the name originally appeared on records as early as 1745, when a landowner named William Stith asked leave of the Council of Virginia to increase his Poplar Forest holdings to 4,000 acres, and in 1749, to 6,000. It is not known if Stith named the property Poplar Forest, but it would have been a natural choice. Tulip poplar trees (*Liriodendron tulipifera*), a species belonging to the magnolia family and native to Virginia, dominated the then-uncleared woodlands. Jefferson once called the tree "the Juno of our groves."

The route that Jefferson took to travel to Poplar Forest in Bedford County lay ninety miles from Charlottesville and less than fifteen miles from Lynch's Ferry, which was founded as the town of Lynchburg in 1786, on lands belonging to John Lynch. Not far away lay three other small towns. One, named Liberty (later Bedford City), became the county seat and Rustburg became the county seat of nearby Campbell County.

The third, New London, established as a town in 1757, played an important role during the Revolutionary War. An armory (later removed) was established there during the war to supply cartridges and repair arms for the Continental Army. The nearby Oxford Iron Works made iron for the military armaments so desperately needed by the colonial troops. Another New London distinction was the court house, the first built in Bedford County (1772), which was to become the backdrop for a celebrated court trial known as the Johnny Hook case that featured the then-young lawyer, Patrick Henry.

Hook was a wealthy Scottish merchant with Tory inclinations who made a great profit from the Revolution. In 1789, Hook sued the army commissary in the district court at New London for a sum of money he claimed was owed him for beef he had supplied to the troops. Patrick Henry's eloquent denunciation of Hook's

Illustration of slave quarters, based on archaeological evidence.

From the Collections of Thomas Jefferson's Poplar Forest. Illustration by Edmund Potter.

profiteering stirred the audience to patriotic fervor. He described the suffering of the Colonial Army and summarized with a dramatic account of the Yorktown campaign. Cries of "Liberty!" rang out in the court room, followed by shouts of "John Hook, beef! beef! beef!" The humiliated Scottish merchant bolted for the door in defeat.

A promising, exciting future lay ahead for Thomas Jefferson—husband, father, landowner, and delegate to the Virginia House of Burgesses. Construction on his mountaintop home, Monticello, was still underway, and Poplar Forest, the property he and Martha had inherited, continued as a working farm, with an overseer in charge of the agriculture and other farm activities.

Jefferson felt encouraged that the profits from his Poplar Forest land would add to his yearly income. Optimistic by nature, the young burgess from Albemarle must have anticipated the future.

Overall, he had reason to be pleased with the direction of his personal and political life. He was unaware of the dark clouds of trouble that, at times, would bring sorrow to him and his family, would change the course of his life and challenge his mind, heart, and spirit.

Bill Barker, interpreter of Thomas Jefferson at Colonial Williamsburg, admires the peaceful Poplar Forest retreat.

Photograph by the author.

CHAPTER 3

ESCAPE TO POPLAR FOREST

We hold these truths to be self-evident: that all men are created equal, that they are endowed by their Creator with certain inalienable rights; that among these are life liberty, and the pursuit of happiness.

From *Declaration of Independence*,
Philadelphia, July 1776

For some months after Jefferson returned to Monticello following his first visit to Poplar Forest in September 1773, he enjoyed relative calm before becoming embroiled in the continuing quarrel between the colonies and England.

In his *Farm Book*, he jotted down a progress report of the ongoing construction at Monticello. Bricks were still being made and fired for his mansion, and at least one of the four "roundabout" roads he planned for the property was ready for use. He remained on his mountaintop while Martha awaited the birth of their second child. Born April 3, 1774, the infant was named Jane Randolph after her grandmother. During his leisure time, Jefferson oversaw the planting of fruit trees, and even helped sow seeds in his vegetable garden, adding numbering sticks to identify the various beds.

Those peaceful months at Monticello were like a tranquil lake before a storm. When Jefferson returned to Williamsburg, the House of Burgesses was in an uproar. Among other injustices, England was continuing to levy taxes and heavy import duties on all goods received at American ports.

Angry colonists carried out acts of defiance that infuriated England and fanned the smoldering embers of revolution. One of the strongest shows of open rebellion had been the Boston Tea Party in 1773, when colonial rebels boarded British ships anchored in the Boston harbor in Massachusetts and dumped chests of British tea overboard in protest against the tax on tea and the East India Company's monopoly on the tea trade.

The British reacted quickly with the closing of the port of Boston. Jefferson met secretly with the other burgesses on May 5, 1774, at Raleigh Tavern in Williamsburg to plan a course of action. Jefferson proposed a resolution *to set aside a day of fasting, humiliation, and prayer to implore heaven to avert from us the evils of civil war.* The Resolution was generally approved, but for political reasons of his own, the Royal Governor, Lord Dunmore, immediately dissolved the assembly.

Later, at Monticello, Jefferson began to scribble down thoughts and ideas to present at a convention that was to meet in Williamsburg in August 1774. He based his writing on his own broad study of history (especially European), politics, government and other related subjects He combined his knowledge of political philosophers, law, and the past history of government with his own ideas, thinking, and reasoning. In part, he wrote: *the colonists should obey only the laws adopted by their own legislatures,* and he advocated an end to all trade with Britain until the port of Boston was reopened, taxes repealed, and restrictions removed on manufacturing and trade.

Apparently, his twenty-three page paper entitled *A Summary View of the Rights of British America,* was read aloud before the group. It was applauded by some; much criticized by others. In time, copies of

Jefferson's *Summary View* were passed from hand to hand, causing escalating excitement among readers, especially when they read words about not only the rights of Americans but of all people everywhere. A press in Williamsburg printed the document in 1774, but Jefferson did not add his name as the author. Later, it was printed in Philadelphia and then in England. The widely read paper added to Jefferson's reputation in small political circles as a skillful writer and may have helped prepare him for the writing of the Declaration of Independence.

The thunder of war grew louder after Patrick Henry's fiery "liberty or death" speech at the Virginia Convention that met in Richmond in March 1775. In fact, after British troops skirmished with colonial militiamen at Concord and Lexington in Massachusetts, the Continental Congress declared a state of defense and chose George Washington to serve as the Commander-in-Chief of the Continental Army.

Over a year later, June 7, 1776, Jefferson met with other members of the Continental Congress in Philadelphia. In a drastic move toward championing colonial rights, a resolution presented by Richard Henry Lee on behalf of the Virginia delegates stated *that the United Colonies should dissolve all allegiance to the British Crown and that all political connection between them & the State of Britain is, & ought to be, totally dissolved.*

On June 11, a committee of five was appointed to draft a Declaration of Independence. The five men selected were Thomas Jefferson, John Adams, Benjamin Franklin, Roger Sherman, and Robert Livingston. They met to discuss the content of the Declaration and to decide which man should do the writing. Although Jefferson at age thirty-three was the youngest, the others respected his writing skills and asked him to prepare the first draft.

Jefferson wrote the document between June 11 and June 28 in the sweltering summer heat in his temporary living quarters on the second floor of a three-story brick house on Market Street that belonged to a young bricklayer named Graaf. Despite the discomforts, Jefferson worked steadily in an upstairs parlor, hunched over the folding writing-box he had designed and asked a skilled Philadelphia cabinetmaker to construct for his use. He wrote rapidly, relying on his quick mind, literary ability, and his personal opinions about freedom and patriotism.

He also depended on his years of extensive reading of philosophy and political history. It is thought that he was especially influenced by the book *Two Treatises on Government* written by John Locke, the English social philosopher and political thinker, whose ideas on natural rights and representative government were somewhat similar to his own. In answer to critics who questioned some of the sources of his ideas in writing the Declaration, Jefferson claimed no originality for the Declaration of Independence and said that his aim was *to place before mankind the common sense of the subject, in terms so plain and firm as to command their assent.*

After he had revised the pages of the Declaration to his satisfaction, Jefferson asked Benjamin Franklin and John Adams to read it for content and to correct mistakes in spelling and grammar. They made minor changes and suggestions, and on June 28 he and the other committee members turned over the rough draft to Congress. According to accounts, the delegates meeting in the State House (known today as Independence Hall) literally debated the document line by line. They deleted words, sentences, and even entire paragraphs, including Jefferson's statement criticizing King George III for imposing the slave trade on the colonies. Jefferson was hurt and understandably upset by some of the changes made in his manuscript, but he remained silent.

Finally, on July 4, delegates from twelve colonies approved the document. New York did not vote its approval until July 15. Nevertheless, the Continental Congress ordered that the Declaration of Independence be printed on handbills and sent to units of the army and to towns and hamlets all over the country in an effort to share it with all Americans.

On July 8, the Declaration was read to a cheering crowd of 3,000 in the State House yard. Bells pealed from church steeples, soldiers marched, and people celebrated. It was July 19 before the document had been engraved on parchment and signed by some of the delegates. By that time many of the men had returned to their homes in the various colonies, and it was months before all of them got to sign it. At first, the public did not recognize Jefferson as its author, and he did not add his signature until August 2.

After the Declaration was signed, proclaiming independence from Great Britain, Jefferson was eager to return to Virginia. He had decided to give up his seat in Congress and requested that his name as a candidate be withdrawn. The letter was late reaching the Virginia convention and though re-elected, he found a replacement. After leaving Philadelphia behind, Jefferson reached Monticello on September 9, 1776.

At first he rejoiced in being with his family, away from the demands of public office, in exchange for the leisurely life of a gentleman farmer on his beloved plantation. At the same time, he was unable to ignore his conscience or to escape from a nagging sense of duty that urged him to continue to serve his country and his native state.

In fact, Jefferson was home only a few weeks before he left to attend the opening of the Virginia General Assembly. That October he took a seat in the Virginia House of Delegates. Without delay he plunged into the work of legislative reform and helped to re-write the entire code of laws that had been written to form the foundation for a strong republican form of government.

Among his proposals was a law that would ban the future importation of slaves to America and legislation to improve education. Both were disregarded. As a member of the committee on religion, he formed a bill that would guarantee religious freedom for all, but ten years passed before his resolution became law in 1786. The passage of the bill not only granted complete freedom of worship to citizens, it abolished all requirements to contribute to the Church of England. Jefferson was to consider the *Virginia Statute of Religious Freedom* to be one of his three major accomplishments of his lifetime and an important contribution to his country's welfare.

From 1776 to 1779, Jefferson continued to submit a barrage of bills and proposals for reform. In the midst of his political responsibilities, his wife Martha, who had been ill for some time, gave birth to a healthy baby girl in August of 1778. They named the child Mary but more often called her Maria or Polly. She and her older sister Patsy were to be the only two of the six children born to the Jefferson's in their ten years of marriage to reach adulthood. Their second daughter, Jane Randolph, had lived only eighteen months.

On June 1, 1779, when Jefferson was thirty-six years old, he was elected Governor of Virginia. The old inner battle began between preferring home and family versus his desire to continue serving in public office. Paradoxically, after less than a month on the job, he thought of the freedom and joy of being at Monticello and wished himself back. He wrote to his family: *The hours of private retirement to which I am drawn by my nature...will be the most welcome of my life.* Yet, in 1780, he accepted re-election for a second term. The Virginia constitution permitted governors to serve one year, but if re-elected, they could remain in office for three consecutive terms.

The following year he was again honored when he was elected a member of the prestigious American Philosophical Society, established in Philadelphia for the promotion of useful knowledge. The following year he was asked to be a member of the Society's council, along with such prominent and distinguished men as George Washington, Marbois, and James Madison.

In March of 1781, the Virginia government was moved from Williamsburg to Richmond, a more central location with less danger of attack from the British. Still, trouble besieged Jefferson from every side. Inflation made money worthless and after a few minor victories in the war, he saw that overall, things were not going well for the field troops. Many colonial militiamen were ill fed and suffered from depression and low morale. They were aware of their lack of training and that they had no choice but to go into battles with inadequate and inferior equipment.

When possible, Jefferson helped provide food and livestock from his Poplar Forest plantation. In one instance, a clerk in the Campbell County Court in Rustburg recorded that "Thomas Jefferson furnished three hundred and twenty-five pound of Beef for which he is allowed at the rate of sixteen shillings and eight pence per Hundred Weight and two pecks of corn for which he is allowed the sum of one shilling." Throughout the Revolution, many other farmers and planters in the colonies sold produce to the army for low prices to help feed the troops.

During his two terms as war-governor, Jefferson tried against almost overwhelming odds to help bring victory to the colonial army. Through correspondence and in secret sessions, he supported military commanders in their combat strategies against Great Britain's powerful, well-armed fighting men.

The war raged on with no early end in sight. Harsh criticism and attacks on Jefferson's handling of the office of governor grew louder. When his term ended on June 2, 1781, Jefferson retired from office. Earlier, he had announced his unwillingness to serve a third term, stating that he was *unprepared by his line of life and education for the command of armies.*

The General Assembly delayed electing his successor as governor, a delay caused by threats of a British invasion of Richmond. The members of the legislature made a timely escape to Charlottesville but, still in retreat, did not take time to vote until, according to plan, they would meet again in Staunton, Virginia.

Meanwhile, Jefferson, considering himself a private citizen and his term officially ended, stayed on at Monticello—at his own risk. In a surprise move at the end of May, 1781, Cornwallis ordered Lieutenant Banastre Tarleton to raid Charlottesville with a party of cavalrymen and mounted infantrymen in a daring attempt to capture members of the General Assembly—and perhaps a special prize: Thomas Jefferson himself.

Except for a certain alert, observant militiaman Captain Jack Jouett, they might have succeeded. On Sunday evening, June 3, Captain Jouett was relaxing in Cuckoo Tavern in Louisa County when he overheard parts of a conversation going on at a nearby table where leaders of a British dragoon were plotting to "kidnap" the governor of Virginia who they believed was still Thomas Jefferson.

Jouett knew that he must reach Monticello before Tarleton and his men arrived. Familiar with back trails and short cuts, he rode over five miles through rough terrain, arriving at the estate before sunrise. After delivering his message to Jefferson, he rode to Charlottesville to warn the Virginia legislators of the impending danger.

Jefferson first made sure his family escaped safely by carriage to the home of friends, Colonel Cole and his family at their Enniscorthy Plantation, about fourteen miles distant. He later wrote in his diary that he had stayed for some time at Monticello *making arrangements for my own departure.* In fact, he delayed leaving his mountain almost too long, waiting until told by a servant that the enemy were ascending the hill leading to Monticello. He then mounted his swiftest horse and escaped through the woods.

The "arrangements" he referred to in his diary included assorting and collecting the pages of a manuscript he was in the process of writing about his native state, together with other important papers and journals. Only then did he feel free to travel with his family to his Poplar Forest plantation in Bedford County to escape the British raiders.

Tarleton had sent a troop of dragoons, led by a Captain McLeod, to the mountaintop, but was disappointed when he discovered that the prize quarry had escaped. However, Tarleton had ordered the troopers not to burn or plunder Monticello.

During his flight, Jefferson had stopped at Enniscorthy, where he had sent Martha and his children. The Jefferson family accepted the Coles invitation to dinner and then drove on, spending the night at Jopling's Inn on the Rockfish River. The next morning, they stopped at Geddes, the home of friends, Col. Hugh Rose in Amherst, and then on to Poplar Forest. A close friend, William Short, and Jupiter, a slave, accompanied them.

There are various other versions of the story about Jefferson's escape from Tarleton's dragoons, some of them legendary, but some are less credible than this account. Whatever the facts, Jefferson no longer considered himself governor and thus felt free to spend time at Poplar Forest that would one day play an important part in his life as a getaway and as a beloved rural retreat.

Jefferson may have intended to spend only a short time there with his family in 1781, but if so, his plan changed abruptly when he injured himself in a fall from his horse, Caractacus. Though Dr. Brown, a local doctor, assured him that the injury was not serious, he and his family stayed at the plantation for an uncertain number of weeks until he was able to travel without difficulty.

The doctor's orders may have come as a blow. As far as is known, no dwelling place existed on the property other than the overseer's small house and slave cabins. An extended stay with the overseer in the heat of summer without ample living space or privacy would put a strain on everyone, but especially on Martha who was still weak and depressed over the recent death in April of their infant daughter.

During this time of enforced idleness, Jefferson recorded matters related to plantation activities and such details as paying the doctor for two visits regarding his accident, payment for chickens he bought from his slaves, Betty, Pat, Dinah, and Judy, who were his chief suppliers, and notations about buying store-bought sugar and coffee.

More importantly Jefferson continued writing on his *Notes on the State of Virginia.* He had begun the project in response to a letter from the Marquis de Barbe-Marbois, secretary to the French Minister in Philadelphia. Over a year before, the Marquis had written to him, asking that he answer twenty-two questions about Virginia. He had also asked the other colonial governors to answer queries about their own colonies. The topics of the questions included manufacturing, plants, government, politics, laws, geology, animals, birds, and nature in general.

Much of the information Jefferson wrote in his answers was based on his own personal observations of such natural wonders as waterways, minerals, climate, geography and vegetation, animal life, and the overall beauty of his native state.

In his chapter on "Productions Mineral, Vegetable and Animal," Jefferson corrected and refuted the theory of Comte de Buffon, a greatly respected French naturalist, that the native peoples and animals of the American continent were smaller than those in Europe.

In still another chapter, entitled "Cascades," Jefferson described certain caves in Virginia and raved over the beauty of Natural Bridge in Rockbridge County which he had owned since 1774 when, for a mere twenty shillings, he had bought the 157 acre-tract on which the bridge was located. In *Notes*, he described the bridge as *the most sublime of Nature's works...springing as it were up to heaven, the rapture of the spectator is really indescribable.*

Despite the doubtless discomfort of his surroundings and working in cramped quarters, Jefferson composed and re-worked great chunks of the manuscript he hoped to mail to Marbois early in the New Year. He worked tirelessly on other chapters of the manuscript, discussing such diverse subjects as: Population, the Constitution, Aborigines, Laws, Colleges, Buildings and Roads, Weights, and Measures and Money, among others. He also added some of his own personal opinions, offering his philosophical views and outlooks on a variety of topics. Among these were religion, manners, customs, and traditions, including those of Native Americans.

Jefferson did not finish the manuscript during his long stay at Poplar Forest. After the family's return to Monticello in late July, aware of its imperfections, he continued collecting data and making changes. It is thought that his lengthy answers to Marbois's twenty-two questions were in the Frenchman's hands by April of 1782.

He allowed a few close friends to read the copy he kept for himself, but apparently had no immediate plans to have the pages published. In time, he was to change his mind, however, and the manuscript bearing the title *Notes on the State of Virginia* was to become a book, acclaimed for its excellence on both sides of the Atlantic.

Safely back at Monticello, Jefferson had much on his mind, most of it unpleasant. Being of a sensitive nature his entire life, he was deeply pained and insulted by the attacks on his reputation as governor for escaping to Bedford County before a new executive had been elected to succeed him. Since mid-June he had brooded over the unfair charges against his character as outlined in a letter that had been hand-delivered to him while he was recuperating from his injury at Poplar Forest. The charges, drawn up in a resolution by the House of Delegates, included cowardice and misconduct and the call for an inquiry into his general conduct during his second year as governor.

Jefferson had replied to the letter in late July after leaving Poplar Forest, asking for more details regarding the accusations, and almost immediately began to prepare his statement of self-defense. On December 12, he was on hand when the Assembly met and, with grim self-control, tried to hide his resentment against what he considered unfair, ridiculous charges. Standing tall, he read aloud each accusation made against him and then replied as honestly as possible.

When he finished, the House made a public apology for the false charges as springing from ungrounded and "popular rumours." The result was the passing of a unanimous resolution in which the legislators thanked him for his "impartial, upright, and attentive administration whilst in office."

Despite the public apology, Jefferson's bitterness over the false accusations remained with him, and he was more anxious than ever to stay on his mountaintop, free of the stress and strain of political life and public humiliation. Refusing an appointment as one of four peace commissioners to negotiate with Great Britain, he wrote to a fellow legislator: *I have taken my final leave of every thing of that nature, have retired to my farm, my family and books from which I think nothing will ever separate me.*

Despite Jefferson's increasing concern about Martha's worsening health, news that the war had taken a turn in favor of the colonial army helped boost his spirits. With the help of the French fleet, commanded by Admiral Count Francois de Grasse, the leadership of the Marquis de Lafayette in assisting American troops, and a strong move of Washington's army from the north, the hope for victory grew brighter.

When the colonials launched a powerful attack against Cornwallis's troops at Yorktown, Virginia, the British wearied and gradually toppled under the unrelenting assault. Discouraged after the long, trying years of war, Cornwallis saw no hope of winning and surrendered to General George Washington on October 12, 1781, at ceremonies in Yorktown. The surrender came as a kind of miracle to the leaders and fighting men of the American army. The revolutionists had turned near-defeat into victory. Following the surrender, however, the war dragged on for at least a year.

Early in 1782, Jefferson must have been thinking once again of his plantation at Poplar Forest, possibly with nostalgia. Since his extended stay there the previous year with his family, he may have been remembering the beauty and tranquillity and may have begun to make plans for the future.

In his *Garden Book,* his first entry on February 12, 1782, concerned the addition of mostly fruit trees for the orchard and a strawberry patch. He wrote in his journal: *Sent to Poplar For. 6 Apricot trees, 2 large Morellas, 2 Kentish cherries, 2 May Dukes, 2 Carnations, 2 Black hearts, 2 White hearts, 2 Newtown pippings, 2 Russetins, 2 Golden Wildings, & some white strawberries.* Orders to his slave, Jupiter, were to take the plants to Bedford County for planting, giving him money *for ferrge. to Popl For.*

As for Monticello, it was far from finished, but sufficiently so that the mansion impressed the Marquis de Chastellux, a member of the French Academy and a major general in the French army, who visited Jefferson at Monticello in the spring of 1782. The Marquis later described the house as being "in the Italian taste" with interior features such as a library of books and a "saloon" on the first floor with a high vaulted ceiling.

Chastellux also described Jefferson himself: *Let me describe to you a man, not yet forty, tall, and with a mild and pleasing countenance, but whose mind and understanding are ample substitutes for every exterior grace. An American, who without ever have quitted his own country, is at once a musician, skilled in drawing, a geometrician, an astronomer, a natural Philosopher, legislator and statesman.*

Age thirty-nine at the time, Jefferson was in excellent physical and mental health. Sadly, the same could not be said about his wife Martha. In early May of that year, after Chastellux's visit, she had borne her sixth child, another daughter they named Lucy Elizabeth. The parents and other members of the family rejoiced that the baby seemed strong and healthy. In their ten years of marriage, the couple had lost two daughters and one son in infancy or early childhood. Only Lucy Elizabeth, Patsy (Martha), age ten, and Polly (Mary or Maria), age four, remained.

Martha, who had been in frail health for some years, now became dangerously ill. Martha Carr, Jefferson's widowed sister who had moved to Monticello with her six children, helped nurse Martha for three months as well as care for baby Lucy and the two older girls. When Jefferson was not at his wife's side, he was busy writing in a small room near her bed.

Martha died on September 6, 1782. *My dear wife died this day at 11:45 a.m.* Jefferson wrote in his *Account Book.*

According to family letters, just before she died, relatives led him to the library where he sank into a stupor and fainted. When he finally roused, he refused all offers of comfort and, overcome with grief, stayed in his bedroom for three weeks, continuously pacing the floor. Except for his oldest daughter, Martha, who shared his sorrow, he admitted no one.

Existing letters tell us that when he finally left his room, he rode horseback almost incessantly, galloping recklessly at a fast pace along back roads, through woods and up mountain paths. When home, he still refused to allow visitors, spending time only with his children.

At least six weeks passed before Jefferson began to emerge from what he described as *that stupor of mind which had rendered me as dead to the world as she was whose loss occasioned it.*

Gradually, as Jefferson recovered from his deep depression, he felt ready to again face the future. In the meantime, some of his friends, among them James Madison, had been working behind the scenes to find some distraction or incentive to lure Jefferson away from Monticello and from constant reminders of his tragic loss.

The answer came when the delegates in the Continental Congress had voted in November of 1782 to appoint him as one of the

American ministers that included John Adams and Benjamin Franklin, to help negotiate peace with Great Britain following the surrender at Yorktown and the end of hostilities. It was an offer to serve overseas that Jefferson had previously refused to accept prior to Martha's death following his governorship of Virginia and his determination to retire from politics.

Now, he accepted without hesitation, eager to leave the past behind. He had decided to take his oldest daughter Martha with him to France, but in Philadelphia, he received word that the French frigate on which they were to sail was icebound below Baltimore and their passage would be delayed indefinitely.

Another event occurred during the frustrating interim that further delayed the much-anticipated overseas adventure. An important piece of news reached American shores that a provisional peace treaty had been signed in negotiating with Great Britain and that members of Congress had voted on April 1, 1783, to delay his mission. Jefferson was happy to learn of the peace settlement but was in a personal quandary. He returned to Virginia for a time where he busied himself writing proposals for a new constitution for his native state, but restless and disappointed, he returned to Philadelphia, unsure of the direction of his future.

It probably came as welcome news when he learned that he had been elected by the Virginia Assembly to serve a term as a delegate to Congress, beginning in late November of that year. Lonely for his children, he decided to take Martha with him to Philadelphia to continue her schooling while the Congress met in session. However, contrary to his carefully laid plans, when the first Congress met in the fall, it was in Annapolis, a more central location than Philadelphia, and as it developed, sometimes the body assembled in Princeton. Each location was considered a temporary seat of government until a permanent site for the nation's capital would be established after the adoption of a new constitution and the inauguration of George Washington as President of the nation.

Jefferson could not help but worry about Patsy's welfare. He knew the inadvisability of moving her about from place to place and decided to leave her in Philadelphia for continued schooling. He made arrangements for her to stay with a Mrs. Thomas Hopkinson, the widowed mother of a fellow signer of the Declaration of Independence, and a woman of some distinction. He also chose *the best tutors in French, dancing, music, and drawing* to give her opportunities for advanced learning. He was confident that Philadelphia would offer his daughter cultural advantages.

Still, despite his confidence in Mrs. Hopkinson and the overall care of his daughter, he continued to feel concern for her well being and sorely missed her companionship. He wrote to her often during this period and looked forward eagerly to her replies. Though she was only age eleven at the time, he drew up a strict schedule of activities that he asked her to follow from day to day and reminded her in many of his letters that she should always strive to be worthy of his love. Fortunately, their correspondence during this period established a close father-daughter bond between them, and throughout her life Martha did indeed try to earn his love and approval.

Jefferson's term in the Continental Congress and Patsy's stay in Philadelphia came to an abrupt but exciting end on May 7, 1784, when he was appointed as minister plenipotentiary to work with John Adams and Benjamin Franklin negotiating amity and commerce treaties in Europe. Delighted with the prospects of working and living abroad, based in Paris, Jefferson left Annapolis within four days. Though he was not reluctant to end his legislative career, he was later to use the political knowledge he had gained in making important contributions to his own state and to the nation.

In less than a week after the welcome news of his assignment reached him, Jefferson picked up Patsy and her luggage in Philadelphia. He did not hesitate to interrupt her schooling with tutors there, certain that in Europe she would receive a valuable education through travel and exposure to Parisian art and culture. He also made arrangements for two other companions to accompany them to Europe. He sent word to contacts in Virginia to have James

Hemings, one of his house slaves at Monticello he called "servant," to meet him in Philadelphia in preparation for the journey. The other was a young friend named William Short whom he asked to go along as his private secretary.

As for the care of his two younger children, Elizabeth Eppes in Albemarle and her husband Francis reassured him that they would gladly care for Polly and Lucy during his absence. He also arranged through correspondence that Nicholas Lewis and his brother-in-law Francis Eppes would manage and supervise the farm operations at Monticello and at Poplar Forest as well as look after his other landholdings.

In one of the trunks packed in preparation for his exciting new venture, Jefferson included the latest revised and expanded version of his manuscript *Notes on the State of Virginia* that had "swelled nearly to treble bulk" in size. He also packed such oddities as the skin of a large panther, hoping to convince the French naturalist Buffon that animals in America were no smaller than those in the Old World.

Jefferson had decided to sail from Boston, in part because he wanted to explore parts of New England before leaving American shores. He and Martha drove first to New York and then to Boston where they were treated with warm hospitality. They traveled to at least two other states in addition to Massachusetts before sailing from Boston harbor on the *Ceres* on July 5, 1784. Neither Jefferson nor his daughter had any way of knowing that it would be five years before they would leave Europe behind and return to America—and to Virginia.

CHAPTER 4

RETURN TO PUBLIC LIFE

God send you safe to the destined port, continue there in health and happiness, as long as you choose to stay, and waft you back to your native country,where you will always be acceptable to the good and virtuous.

John Tyler to Thomas Jefferson, 1784

The first winter Jefferson spent in France was unusually bleak and cold. Intermittent physical ailments kept him indoors a good deal of the time. An interchange of letters with Patsy and frequent visits with her at the convent school, the Abbaye Royale de Panthemont where she was enrolled, helped lift his spirits and relieve his loneliness and melancholy. Despite his efforts to recover from grief following his wife Martha's premature death, he sometimes gave in to despondency.

In January, something happened that made him feel even more depressed than before. Lafayette brought him the tragic news from Virginia that his youngest child, Lucy Elizabeth, had died from whooping cough. Fortunately, Polly had been spared, but Jefferson mourned the loss of still another of his children.

When the weather warmed, he felt more cheerful. He explored the ancient streets of Paris, browsing in shops and bookstalls. Almost from the beginning of his stay, he rummaged for books, some for present reading, others to send home to friends and some for his future library in Virginia.

Jefferson's main duties as a special envoy in the role of plenipotentiary minister to France were to promote American interests by expanding trade and commerce and working closely with John Adams and Benjamin Franklin in negotiating commercial treaties and trade agreements. He also tried to correct some of the false impressions foreigners had about America (and Americans) and made efforts to repay the financial debt his country owed the French.

In 1785, around the time his first year abroad was ending, Jefferson's life took an unexpected turn. Congress appointed him to succeed Dr. Franklin as minister to France. Franklin, at age 79, was too ill to continue in the post and, at his own request, had asked for and been granted leave to return to America. John Adams had been appointed minister to England.

Two weeks after he received his commission on May 2, Jefferson traveled to Versailles to be presented to Louis XVI. He was received officially as the new minister during an elaborate ceremony. He would spend the next four years stationed in Paris. As the successor to the distinguished Benjamin Franklin, he knew that he had big shoes to fill. It was a daunting challenge. Franklin had been highly respected and popular with the French. As the new American minister, he hoped that in time he, too, would win the acceptance and trust of the French people.

In May of 1785, another important event that occurred in Jefferson's life was the first printing of his *Notes on the State of Virginia* in book form. In the past he had not tried to have the manuscript published, but he found that printing costs in Paris were much lower than in America and he also had more confidence in the manuscript after making corrections and revisions and adding pages, especially to the sections on natural history, using facts and figures he had collected from scientists and naturalists.

He decided to order the printing of two hundred private copies, to be read by a few special friends such as Lafayette, Chastellux, and Buffon. He mailed most of the other copies to his closest friends in America, many of them political colleagues, and for possible distribution to William & Mary students.

Later, he was distressed to learn that a French bookseller had acquired a copy of the book, employed a translator, and was planning to publish an "abominable translation." In an effort to counter the threat, Jefferson authorized an acquaintance from the French Academy, to prepare a translation. When printed, Jefferson considered it second-rate.

Now that the book had become public, he rightfully feared that an inferior English translation of the book might appear in print without his permission. Encouraged by friends, he decided to have 1,000 copies printed by John Stockdale, a reputable English bookseller and publisher. The edition, printed in July 1787, proved to be the basis for all other copies of the book published during Jefferson's lifetime.

Today, *Notes on the State of Virginia* is widely regarded as an important classic and a valuable addition to American letters and science that best expresses Jefferson's knowledge of and the depth of his learning in many fields of study. The book also offers insights into the author's thoughts, personal philosophy, and views. It also acquaints the reader with the scope of his remarkable mind and talents that made (and make) him a distinctive and famous American.

From the beginning of his stay in France, Jefferson was intrigued by the French people of all classes. With a critical eye, he observed their manners, customs, dress, and their different folkways. He did not fail, however, to notice the poverty existing among the country's twenty million people. In protest, he once wrote that great numbers of the French were *more wretched and accursed in every circumstance of human existence than the most conspicuously wretched individual in the whole United States.* He—like many others—put the blame on the French government and on a group of wealthy and powerful leaders who ignored the suffering of the sick and poor.

True to habit, Jefferson continued to record many of his observations in ledgers and journals during his five years in Europe. He

explored small hamlets, towns and cities and the rural countryside. He took notes on French farming practices, methods of industry, new inventions, agriculture, birds, plants, museums and
galleries. He was also interested in such matters as canal locks,
languages and dialects, landscape designs, hot-air balloons, cheese-
making, wine-making, secrets of better crop production, rice-clean-
ing and the different species of rice.

But he was especially fascinated by French art and culture. *Were
I to proceed to tell you how much I enjoy their architecture, sculpture,
painting, music, I should want for words,* he once remarked. *It is in
these arts they shine.*

He took a particular interest in the designs of chateaux and
villas and in the classical architecture of public buildings. At Nimes,
France, he stood speechless before an ancient Roman temple
known as the Maison Quaree built during the first century of the
Christian era. Fascinated with the structure, he studied it carefully,
calling it *one of the most beautiful, if not the most beautiful and precious
morsel of architecture left us by antiquity.*

In fact, his study of the Maison Quaree influenced the plans
and sketches he sent to America in 1786, using the temple as a
model for the Virginia State Capitol in Richmond. In response
to a letter from officials asking him to make renderings of possible architectural styles for the new capitol building in his native state, he concentrated his energies into the challenging
project. Jefferson did not admire the traditional colonial style
so widespread across America. His classical education, his readings of books on ancient architecture and his observations of
buildings in Europe, had given him a love of antiquity and classical architecture.

He secured the services of a well-known French architect,
Charles Louis Clerisseau, with whom he worked closely to prepare the designs for the capitol. It was the first public building in
America to be built in the neoclassical style. "Neo" is a Greek word
that means new; the new classical style looked like the old classical
style of the ancient Romans, combined with new elements and
designs with "a harmony of parts."

The buildings Jefferson admired in France, Italy and other parts of Europe were also to contribute to and influence the changes he would make later at Monticello and to the design of the retreat he would build at Poplar Forest.

Occasional letters from Albemarle and Bedford Counties kept Jefferson somewhat informed about plantation activities. In 1784, a letter to him in Paris from his brother-in-law, Francis Eppes, gave a very bad account of crops at Monticello as well as Bedford. Three years later, in correspondence with Nicholas Lewis, Jefferson suggested that he open more land at Poplar Forest and send more slaves to work there, *as the lands in Bedford are much better for tobacco than those of Albemarle.*

Letters also kept Jefferson in touch with family members in Virginia, including his daughter Polly who, according to her letters, remained happy with her aunt and uncle, Elizabeth and Francis Eppes, at Eppington. In fact, she was so happy there that when her father began urging her to join him and Patsy in Paris, she refused to go. Jefferson wrote to her, saying: *I wish so much to see you, that I have desired your uncle and aunt to send you to me. I know, my dear Polly, how sorry you will be, and ought to be, to leave them and your cousins; but your sister and myself cannot live without you, and after a while we will carry you back again to see your friends in Virginia.*

Polly was not persuaded. In 1785, she wrote:

Dear Papa,

I should be very happy to see you, but I can not go to France, and hope that you and sister Patsy are well. Your affectionate daughter. Adieu.

That was not the end of it. After Jefferson replaced Benjamin Franklin as minister to the French court in 1785, he had been assured of two more years in France. He continued to miss his youngest daughter and was more determined than ever that she must come to Paris, especially so after a romantic relationship with a beautiful and talented young woman, Maria Cosway, ended.

In May, 1786, in another letter of refusal, Polly wrote: *Dear Papa—I long to see you, and hope that you and sister Patsy are well; give my love to her and tell her that I long to see her, and hope that you and she will come very soon to see me. I hope that you will send me a doll. I am very sorry that you have sent for me. I don't want to go to France, I had rather stay with Aunt Eppes, Aunt Carr, Aunt Nancy and Cousin Polly Carr here. Your most happy and dutiful daughter. Polly Jefferson*

As it turned out, Polly had no real choice in the matter. Through letters to Virginia, Jefferson arranged for a guardian to accompany her on a ship sailing the summer of 1787. After two months away from Eppington, she arrived safely in Paris.

Following a week's holiday with her father, Polly often visited Patsy at the convent and, as she adjusted to her new life, attended the same school where she learned to speak and read French with ease, took art lessons, learned to play the harpsichord, and made new friends. Both girls spent as much time as possible with their father who bought them stylish clothes, and introduced them to many of his distinguished friends, as part of his plan to expose them to a new world of art and culture.

Letters from America, especially those from his friend James Madison, brought Jefferson the latest news about happenings in the government. One of the most important pieces of news he received was mention of the meeting in Philadelphia of the Constitutional Convention in May 1787, during which fifty-five delegates busily drafted a constitution that was to replace the old Articles of Confederation.

Though separated by an ocean Jefferson wrote back to express his personal views. Months later, when Madison, an influential leader at the convention, sent him a draft of the proposed constitution, he was troubled by two things: one was that the number of terms a president could serve had not been limited and the other was that it failed to include a Bill of Rights.

In a letter to Madison, Jefferson wrote: *A Bill of Rights is what the people are entitled to, against every government on earth, general or particular, and what no just government should refuse.* His letters helped convince delegates of the importance of adding a Bill of Rights to the document. However, the Constitution was actually drafted *without* a Bill of Rights. Ratification in some states hinged upon the promise of the addition of a Bill of Rights statute by the first Congress. These ten amendments were written in 1789 and ratified by 1791. This much-admired document contained the principles and laws that constituted a new federal system of government.

Meanwhile in Paris, hordes of French people were protesting loudly against the great divisions that continued to exist between the rich and poor. Jefferson wrote to a friend in Virginia that the common people in France suffered *under physical and moral oppression,* and he feared that the poverty and inequalities could lead to a Revolution.

Jefferson had kept in close touch with his friend Lafayette and discussed with him and others the need for gradual change and reform. Because of his position as a diplomat, he dared not speak out publicly. Instead, he involved himself with a small group of French leaders who were trying to work out differences and to guarantee individual rights that would eliminate most of the unfair privileges reserved for the rich aristocratic class.

The ruling powers, however, continued to ignore the masses and their demands until, finally, it was too late. Hordes of angry oppressed people rioted in the streets, and as the rebellion gathered force, it turned into a bloody revolution. In July 1789, furious rebels stormed and occupied the Bastille, a fortress in Paris used as a prison.

Jefferson described the scene in a letter to John Adams, who had been appointed U.S. Minister to London: He wrote, in part, that *in the course of three months, the royal authority has lost, and the rights of the nation gained as much ground by a revolution.*

By August of 1789, the French had in place a new national assembly and had adopted a new social philosophy with a document entitled the *Declaration of the Rights of Man and Citizen.* Lafayette, who much admired the American Declaration of Independence, had drafted the declaration.

During a period of relative calm in Paris in 1788, Jefferson wrote to the American Congress in November, asking for a six-month leave of absence to return to Virginia. He was concerned about his farms and other affairs after such a long absence, and he thought it wise to remove his daughters from the convent for a time and return to America.

It was August of the next year before Jefferson learned that his request for a leave to return home toAmerica had been granted. The Jefferson family sailed from Le Havre across the channel to England on October 7. Two weeks later, they boarded the *Clermont* bound for Norfolk, Virginia, and reached American soil on November 23, 1789. Jefferson had been away from Virginia and his native land for over five years.

Soon after they arrived and disembarked, Jefferson received an unsettling piece of news. President George Washington had nominated him to serve as his secretary of state and the Senate had already confirmed it.

The offer did not elate a weary Jefferson. He found the proposition somewhat bewildering, even troubling. According to his plans for the future, he had hoped to return to Paris after his leave to give his support to Lafayette, and in his own words, *see the end of the Revolution.* Afterward, he had planned to leave France, return home to America and his beloved Virginia, and officially, as he said openly, *withdraw from political life, to sink into the bosom of my family and friends, and to devote myself to studies more congenial to my mind.*

In the midst of his personal turmoil, Patsy, at age seventeen, announced her engagement to be married. Though Jefferson knew he would miss her greatly, he gave his consent. He praised her fiancée, Thomas Mann Randolph, Jr., describing him as *a young man of genius, science, and honorable mind.*

The marriage took place on February 23, 1790, at Monticello. Thereafter, it is likely that he began to call her Martha rather than her childhood name, Patsy, in recognition of her new status and maturity. Existing copies of letters between father and daughter show that he had begun to address her as "My dear Martha," or "My Dear Daughter."

As part of her dowry, Martha's father gave her a tract of 1000 acres of Poplar Forest land in Bedford that he described as *my best plantation.* What he considered his "best plantation" was a tract known as Wingo's located near the westernmost boundary of Poplar Forest. Besides the gift of land, Jefferson deeded Martha and her heirs twenty-seven slaves and *all the stock of work horses, cattle, hogs & sheep & the plantation interests now on or belonging to the plantation called Wingo's.*

Jefferson continued to sway back and forth on the matter of serving as Washington's secretary of state. Should he accept or refuse?

In the end, pressure from Madison, and especially from President Washington, helped him make up his mind. In mid-February of 1790, he wrote to the President, accepting the post that had been set up under the new government.

By the time the First Congress ended in March 1791, no definite political parties had yet been formed. Even though Washington gave Alexander Hamilton, his secretary of the treasury, more authority in decision-making than to any other member of his cabinet, a group in the legislature united to oppose Hamilton's policies. During the Second Congress, Jefferson was the leader of the anti-Hamilton group that became the Democratic-Republican Party. An opposing bloc, made up mainly of Hamilton supporters, formed the Federalist Party.

As the unofficial leader of the Democratic-Republican Party, Jefferson emphasized limited government and a government that represented all the people. He and his followers also believed in less government and more freedom for the individual.

In contrast, the members of the Federalist Party supported the idea of a strong central government, dependent on the rich for its strength. Rival Democratic-Republicans accused John Adams, Washington's vice president, of being the "advocate for hereditary powers" that defended titles and ranks.

As department heads in Washington's cabinet, Jefferson and Hamilton became bitter rivals. They disagreed and clashed on matters of finance, foreign and domestic policy, the interpretation of the Constitution and other controversial issues. They criticized one another privately and publicly.

On the positive side, the nation's capital was to be moved from New York to Philadelphia. Jefferson looked forward to the move.

He was often lonely in New York as he admitted in a letter to Martha: *Having had yourself & dear Poll to live with me so long, to exercise my affections and cheer me in the intervals of business, I feel heavily the separation from you.*

Among his accomplishments as secretary of state was the drafting of a report in which he proposed the application of the standard decimal system to weights and measures, just as, at his recommendation, had been done earlier with coinage. Another was his invention of the wheel cipher that was used to encode and decode messages as a facet of American foreign policy. Additionally, while in office, he sponsored the first patent law in the nation. Once the bill was approved, inventors could apply for protection of their work.

On September 1, 1790, after Congress adjourned, Jefferson, accompanied by Madison, set out for Monticello in Jefferson's phaeton carriage. They stopped in Philadelphia where Jefferson made arrangements for his office and living quarters in preparation for the move from New York. They also stopped in Georgetown on the Potomac to examine a tract of land that was being considered as the permanent site for the nation's future capitol.

George Washington also stopped there on his way to Mount Vernon. Later, in a discussion with the President, Jefferson encouraged Washington to act quickly to obtain the land, appoint experts to design detailed layouts of the proposed seat of government, and even begin to plan for the construction of the first buildings. President Washington asked Jefferson to serve as an unofficial assistant in planning the still-unnamed city. Jefferson wrote to Major Pierre Charles L'Enfant, a French-born architect in America, to formulate original drawings. In the letter, he expressed his own preference, saying: *I should prefer the adoption of some one of the models of antiquity which have had the approbation of thousands of years.*

Jefferson played an important part in locating, planning, developing, and making suggestions for building designs and construction. He is also credited with giving the name Washington to what was to become the nation's first permanent capitol. It was to be located on a ten-mile-square strip of land, part of it a swamp, lying between a for-est and the Potomac River. He put his observations of architecture in Europe to good use in assisting with building designs and recommend-ing wide, spacious, tree-lined streets and other landscaping details that would enhance the beauty of the Federal City.

The New Year, 1791, began on a happy note. Martha Jefferson Randolph gave birth to her first child, Anne Cary, who was born at Monticello on January 23. Jefferson was delighted to become a grandfather, and after five years in France, to be back home and easily accessible to family members and friends. He realized how homesick he had actually been for Virginia and for the familiar plantation life at Monticello. He was also happy to see his daugh-ters reach adulthood in their own country. Martha was now a busy young mother and Polly was living temporarily with her aunt and uncle at Eppington.

After two years as Secretary of State, administering domes-tic and foreign affairs, Jefferson grew weary. He was tired of coping with endless disagreements with Hamilton, of the end-less political infighting, and of Congressional opposition to some of his ideas related to the construction of the national capital. Another reason for the increasing worries and job stress was the renewed outbreak of the seemingly never-ending war be-tween Britain and France. Though his term was not over, he decided to write a letter to President Washington asking to re-sign in good standing.

Washington refused to approve Jefferson's first request to re-sign, insisting that he stay in office at least another year, until the end of 1793. Later, James Madison joined the President in urging him to remain in office to make "a further sacrifice of your longings for the repose of Monticello."

The next year, September 12, 1792, Martha gave birth to Thomas Jefferson Randolph, Jefferson's namesake, who would one day take over the management of his Albemarle and Bedford County properties. The joy and excitement of having grandchildren of his own only added to Jefferson's desire for a definite end to public service and the freedom to return to

Monticello to stay. In a letter to a neighbor, he said that *the fine sunshine of Albemarle seems made for all the world but me.*

Later that summer, a plague of yellow fever in Philadelphia drove thousands from the city. Jefferson left for Monticello in September. During the reprieve he took time to reacquaint himself with plantation life and to play with his first two grandchildren, but in November he returned sadly to his office. Political intrigue had not lessened, and at intervals he suffered from headaches so severe that he had to take to his bed. In a letter to his daughter Martha, he wrote, *I become more and more disgusted with the jealousies, the hatred, the rancorous and malignant passion of this scene, and lament my having ever again been drawn into public view.*

Jefferson resigned officially as Secretary of State on the last day of the year in 1793. On January 5, soon after George Washington reluctantly accepted his resignation, he wrote to his daughter Polly that he expected to be home by the middle of the month, *no more to leave you.*

When Jefferson returned to Monticello as a private citizen, he was determined to leave government service behind forever. Fortunately for the young nation, that did not occur. In his desire to help establish a sound democratic form of American government, Jefferson was to be lured back to the public arena.

Busy months followed at Monticello. Not long after leaving Philadelphia, Jefferson wrote to George Washington, saying that he had returned to farming *with an ardor which I scarcely knew in my youth, and which has got the better entirely of my love of study.*

Back in 1790, when he had agreed to become Secretary of State, Jefferson had asked Nicholas Lewis to continue supervising his properties in both Albemarle and Bedford. However, soon after his return, he realized that his farms needed his personal attention. During his ten-year absence, poor farming practices had lowered production.

During this period of renewal at Monticello, Jefferson helped welcome his third grandchild into the world on October 13, 1796. The infant was a baby girl, Ellen Wayles Randolph, who would one day become a favorite granddaughter and Jefferson's frequent companion during visits to Poplar Forest. That same eventful year marked another important family milestone. His younger daughter, Polly, beautiful at age eighteen, married John Wayles Eppes at Monticello. Jefferson approved of the match. As a wedding gift, he deeded to the couple his nearby Pantops plantation where he hoped to someday build a house for them on the property.

He began rebuilding parts of Monticello and added innovations he had seen in Europe, such as skylights, alcove beds, and indoor privies. He also changed or adapted devices invented by others for additional comfort and convenience.

During his years away from home, Jefferson had depended on letters to stay in touch with his various overseers regarding the agriculture and overall care of his landholdings. Now, at Monticello he could assist in overseeing the rotation of crops and the tilling of the soil with the *moldboard plow of least resistance* he had designed in 1788. Jefferson described the plow as *mathematically demonstrated to be perfect.* Its main advantages were that it needed less force to pull than other plows and could easily be duplicated.

Jefferson also supervised the building of a threshing machine from a model sent to him from England by Thomas Pinckney. The horse-powered machine, first used in the 1796 harvest, could be carried from field to field.

Demands of one kind or another at Monticello caused him to cancel a planned visit to Poplar Forest. He had been pleased to receive an encouraging letter from Bowling Clark, his then-overseer in Bedford, stating that he and the other workers were *managing uncommonly well* and that wheat was selling at a good price in Richmond. The only discouraging news at the time was that "measles is among your Negroes at Bedford, but they have lost none."

Other letters from his Poplar Forest plantation brought him news of small profits from the sale of scanty crops that had been hurt by spells of unseasonably cold weather, or by too much rain, or severe droughts during several successive growing seasons. One year Jefferson wrote in his Farm Book that *unlike the field crops, the*

livestock at Bedford was flourishing. Eighty-three hogs had been slaugh-
tered; five went to his overseer Bowling Clark, five to the slaves, and the
rest were sent to Monticello.

Letters also kept Jefferson in touch with the outside world. At
age fifty-three and in excellent health, he reveled in his country
squire role. There were letters from former allies in government,
telling him about the latest happenings; and a few tried to per-
suade him to re-enter politics. In fact, certain Democratic-Republican supporters who believed in a decentralized national government, began urging him to run for president to succeed George
Washington who had refused to run for a third term.

Jefferson wrote back, saying that he had *no ambition to govern*
men. Still, while he did not campaign for the office, he did not stop
his supporters from working behind the scene to endorse him as a
likely rival to run against John Adams, the candidate for the Federalist Party. Though Jefferson and Adams had been good friends
for many years, the differences in their party views had gradually
soured their friendship.

Jefferson was relieved when Adams was elected president
with 71 electoral votes to his 68. However, according to the Constitution, the candidate with the next highest vote automati-
cally became vice president. The two leaders were inaugurated
on March 4, 1797.

That same month and year, Jefferson was installed as president of the American Philosophical Society, of which he had been
a member and councilor for some years. A week later, he presented a paper on the fossil remains of a huge animal recently
discovered in the western part of Virginia. Jefferson felt honored
to be elected president of the prestigious Society.

He once said of himself: *Nature intended me for the tranquil*
pursuits of science, by rendering them my supreme delight. But the
enormities of the times in which I have lived, have forced me to take
part in resisting them, and to commit myself on the boisterous ocean of
political passions.

CHAPTER 5

IN THE DRIVER'S SEAT

*This summer will entirely finish the house at Monticello
& I am preparing an occasional retreat in Bedford, where
I expect to settle some of my grandchildren.*

Jefferson to Elizabeth Trist, a friend from
Philadelphia, 1806

Soon after taking office in 1797 as vice president, Jefferson was pleased to discover that he had far fewer duties and responsibilities than as secretary of state. The vice president's main duty was to preside over the meetings of the United States Senate. He became adept at doing so and compiled a manual of parliamentary procedure. In his role as the leader of the Democratic-Republican Party, he continued his efforts to limit and control the mushrooming growth and power of the Federalists.

In turn, influential Federalists made vicious attacks against him as vice president, both in the press and by other stealthier means. Critics slandered his character and questioned his fitness as a national leader. The accusations and lies hurt deeply. In letters to his daughters and friends, Jefferson admitted to being embittered by such traits in humans as envy, hatred and the jealousy and malice he encountered in government circles.

Jefferson made valiant efforts to defend himself and his principles of good government. In letters, at public meetings, and in
private discussions, he stressed the importance of the Constitution and the rights and powers of states apart from *the general government or executive branch.*

He (and like-minded Democratic-Republicans) believed that
the government should be run in a "rigorously frugal and simple"
manner. He also believed in free commerce with all nations, but
with "political connection with none," and he repeatedly stressed
the importance of freedom of the press and religion.

When Congress adjourned on May 15, 1800, Jefferson went
home for most of the summer to escape Philadelphia's heat and
humidity. By letter, he kept in touch with his cabinet officers and
departmental chief clerks.

During this period, Jefferson decided to take a long-delayed
trip to Poplar Forest. Soon after he arrived, wind began to howl
around the overseer's house where he was staying. Thunder rattled
and roared, and lightning forked the sky. Rain spewed down, spit-
ting at windows and doors. It rained for three days. Almost the
entire time, Jefferson was cooped up with the Clark family, including children and dogs, in a small house lacking privacy and
quiet. All he could find to read in the household was an almanac.
He occupied some of his idle time estimating the amount of the
national debt and how best to pay it.

In a letter written in retrospect many years later, one of his
granddaughters, Ellen Randolph, wrote that the visit might have
encouraged Jefferson *to think seriously of building a house at Poplar
Forest.* Indeed, his three-day stay in the crowded house during a
rainstorm could have rekindled his long-held desire to build an
uninterrupted retreat for the solitary study of high problems.

The idea of building a retreat for himself began years before, at
least as early as 1781, when as ex-governor, Jefferson and his family
had spent five weeks or more in hiding at Poplar Forest after he had
eluded Tarleton's dragoons during the struggle for independence.

For that matter, there is reason to believe that the idea of having a private retreat kept surfacing at different periods during his

life. In 1786, Jefferson had written from Paris to a friend, saying: *I sometimes think of building a little hermitage at the Natural Bridge (for it is my property) and of passing there a part of the year at least.*

His dream of a hideaway also may have been fostered during his years in France when he had stayed at brief intervals with an order of French lay brothers who had established a hermitage on the mountain of Mont Calvaire. According to later recollections by his daughter Martha, her father had left his duties as French minister "whenever he had a press of business" to spend a week or more at the hermitage. There, with other paying guests, he could relax, enjoy the fresh air, the magnificent beauty of the surroundings, and his friendship with the brothers.

In his later years, Jefferson had additional reasons for wanting a hideaway of his own. He yearned at times to leave his political worries behind and to escape from the overflow crowds of visitors that continued to flock to Monticello. In addition to his resident sister, Martha and her six children, more friends, acquaintances, and relatives than ever imposed on his hospitality (and pocketbook), expecting to be fed well, housed, and entertained. It was not unusual for one-day visits to extend to a week or longer. Even strangers came out of curiosity, hoping to see famed Thomas Jefferson and his home.

When Jefferson left Virginia in November of 1800, to finish his term as vice president, he did not return to Philadelphia. Instead, he traveled to Washington, to see the new Federal City along the Potomac still under construction.

Adams was finishing his term as the second president. Nationwide, re-electing the incumbent candidate or electing a new president was a topic of conversation. The Democratic-Republican candidates for president and vice president were Thomas Jefferson and Aaron Burr. Their opponents were Federalists John Adams and Charles Cotesworth Pinckney.

Although Jefferson had refused to campaign for the presidency, groups of his friends, especially those who were Democratic-Republicans, tried to convince him that he owed it to the country—and to himself—to run for the office. The persuasion and encouragement worked; he finally agreed to run as his party's candidate.

Even though John Adams' overall popularity as president had lessened during his term in office, analysts predicted a close contest. The count of electoral votes showed a tie between Jefferson and Burr, since the Constitution had not provided for separate elections for these two offices. The House of Representatives chose Jefferson over Burr, making him the third President of the United States. Aaron Burr was his vice president.

Jefferson was fifty-seven years old when he gave his inaugural address on March 4, 1801, in the Senate chamber of the Capitol. *A good government is a wise and frugal government which shall restrain men from injuring one another,* he said in part, *which shall leave them otherwise free to regulate their own pursuits of industry and improvement, and shall not take from the mouth of labor the bread it has earned.*

Soon after Inauguration Day, Jefferson moved from his boardinghouse into the tan sandstone President's House. The slate roof leaked and some walls were still unplastered, but he was used to living at Monticello, his still-unfinished house.

When he became tense, the new president sometimes went outdoors to do manual labor, cutting down a wilderness of bushes, briars, weeds, and scrubby grasses that still surrounded the White House. *When my head starts to spin with too much thought, I can steady it up with five minutes of gardening,* he once told James Madison.

Ultimately, his feeble efforts to clear the entanglements were hopeless. When Congress did not appropriate money for landscaping, Jefferson paid part of his $25,000 annual salary to hardworking landscape gardeners.

Another of his diversions was watching and listening to his favorite mockingbird that he kept in a nearby cage. It is said that when released, the bird sometimes mimicked the songs of woodland birds and perched on one or another of Jefferson's shoulders. Sometimes it even nibbled crumbs of food from his lips.

Throughout his years as president, Jefferson continued, as was his habit, to put comfort before style in his dress. He often wore a shabby brown coat and corduroy breeches and an old red waistcoat. However, for government and social affairs he wore fashionable clothes to fit the occasion.

Gray had begun to streak his faded reddish hair, but his hazel-colored eyes were still clear and intelligent. Though he could hardly have been called handsome, many people were impressed by his simple, informal ways.

In choosing his cabinet, Jefferson emphasized loyalty, knowledge and wisdom. As chief executive, he tried not to dominate others or always insist on having his own way. Still, he let members of Congress know that he was in command.

As President, he worked long hours. Arising at 5 A.M., he concentrated on finishing his deskwork by nine o'clock. Meetings with cabinet members and other officials followed, usually until noon. On most days, for exercise and diversion, he rode horseback for at least an hour. He often worked until 10 at night or attended government social functions. Throughout his years in public office, and especially as president, Jefferson's main goal was to make democracy work so well that it might become a model for good government in other parts of the world.

During his first term, Jefferson's most important achievement was the Louisiana Purchase. Through diplomats in his foreign service, he learned that a vast expanse of land ceded to Spain in 1763 had been given back to France. He also learned that Napoleon Bonaparte, who then controlled France, was interested in selling New Orleans and the Floridas (especially west Florida) to the United States. Jefferson felt certain that such an acquisition would help assure America's future growth and prosperity.

Early in 1803, Jefferson nominated James Monroe to serve as a special emissary to work with Robert Livingston, the United States minister to France, in negotiating a shrewd deal. The Senate confirmed his nomination.

Monroe arrived in Paris on April 12 to find that Livingston had been rebuffed at every turn, but later was astounded to hear of a totally unexpected event. The previous day, before his arrival, Livingston had been requested to report to the office of Tallyrand, the French foreign minister, who proceeded to ask him an amazing question: *Would the United States be interested in purchasing All of Louisiana?* Livingston learned that earlier on the morning of April 11, in a discussion with his finance minister, Barbe-Marbois, Napoleon had announced his decision to sell all of Louisiana to the United States.

Monroe and Livingston succeeded so well in the negotiations that they were able to draw up a tentative treaty for the purchase of the territory of Louisiana. The boundaries were to be the same as when transferred from Spain to France. The two Americans initialed the agreement and on May 2 they signed the treaty that ceded the entire territory to the United States. The price tag was fifteen million dollars.

Jefferson was aware, however, of a major obstacle that could forestall the Senate's approval and confirmation of the purchase. The constitution did not give the government the power to hold foreign territory or incorporate it into the Union. Known as a strict constructionist, Jefferson thought, in principle, that the Constitution should be interpreted in an exact way and that a constitutional amendment was necessary for the legal annexation of Louisiana to the United States.

He faced a dilemma. In messages from Paris, Monroe and Livingston were urging quick action in ratifying the treaty agreement with France. If it was delayed, they feared that Napoleon Bonaparte might change his mind.

Adopting an amendment would take time, too much time. Jefferson and his party colleagues decided to be practical. In consideration of the extraordinary opportunity to acquire so much territory at a bargain price, they agreed to by-pass the constitutional issue, and proceed with the land deal. On July 4, the twenty-seventh birthday of the American nation, Napoleon made the final decision to sell Louisiana to the American nation. The offer did not include the Floridas.

Federalists spoke out vigorously against Jefferson's impressive land acquisition, calling it "a waste of money, "a great curse" and accused him and his supporters of purchasing a "wilderness populated by wolves and Indians."

Overnight, the president's public popularity zoomed, but that did not stop the press from continuing to attack him or keep Federalists from opposing the purchase. Small groups of the opposing party even went so far as to label the transfer of Louisiana to the United States a conspiracy that would help keep Democratic-Republicans in power.

Large numbers of supporters in his own party offered their whole-hearted support of the Purchase, as some came to call the exciting proposition. At the opening of the Eighth Congress, called into early session on October 17, 1803, Jefferson requested the legislators to prepare to finalize the treaty without delay, using all administrative measures necessary to annex Louisiana into the Union. He emphasized that the purchase would provide great tracts of additional agricultural land for the immigrants who continued to populate America. The Senate ratified the treaty to purchase Louisiana on October 20, 1803, by a vote of 24 to 7.

On December 20, of that year France formally transferred Louisiana to the United States at a ceremony in New Orleans. The United States had acquired over 800,000 square miles of land, most of it situated between the Rocky Mountains and the Mississippi river, more than doubling the nation's size.

In early January of 1803, Jefferson had made another bold move. Despite the then-uncertainty of the land transfer, in a confidential message to Congress, he asked for an appropriation of $2,500 to fund *a western expedition in which commercial, scientific, and military objectives would be conjoined.* His plan for the expedition was that explorers would trace the Missouri River to its source, discover a route to the Pacific Ocean, and try to increase trade with the Indian tribes. Congress quietly granted his request. The president signed the legislation on February 28, 1803.

Jefferson already knew the man he wanted to lead the expedition into the newly acquired territory. He had discussed the possible exploration with Meriwether Lewis, his private secretary, and a former army officer from Virginia. In a letter to a friend, he described Lewis as *brave, prudent, habituated to the woods, & familiar with Indian manners and character.*

Lewis chose William Clark, a fellow Virginian, and ex-Army officer, as his co-captain. Lewis began to collect supplies and equipment for the journey. He also read books to increase his knowledge of wilderness living and received training in various skills and fields of study, including map-making, surveying, survival in the wild, nature in all its aspects and the sciences of botany, zoology, astronomy and medicine.

Before the outset of the expedition, President Jefferson instructed the explorers to bring back detailed information and, if possible, living specimens of birds and animals, and to make an assessment of the marine life of lakes and rivers. He also asked them to collect data and samples of trees, shrubs, plants, rocks and minerals, and to make a study of the geography and topography of the land.

Perhaps even more important, Jefferson told Lewis and Clark to try to make friends with and gather extensive information about the fur trappers and Indians who lived in the vast territory. He was vitally interested in the natives. He requested the captains to learn the names of the tribes, the locations of their camps, food, their languages, religions, populations and customs. He also suggested that they draw rough sketches of some of the tribespeople, their dress and ornaments, and if they could, even bring back a real chieftain to visit him in Washington.

Tell the Indians of our wish to be neighborly, friendly, and useful to them, he advised, and *to take along articles of trade they may need or furnish. Ideally, presents for the natives would include such gifts as beads and other ornaments, buttons, medals, cotton shirts, tools, blankets, flags, household utensils, red cloth and tomahawks...the object of your mission is to explore the Missouri river & such principal stream of it, as, by its course and communication with the waters of the Pacific Ocean.*

Lewis and Clark and their Corps of Discovery crew set forth on Monday afternoon May 14, 1804. They traveled up the Missouri River in a keelboat that could be sailed or rowed. They also took along two smaller boats called pirogues. During the journey they added an interpreter, Toussaint Charbonneau, to the crew.

The nationally touring exhibit, *Corps of Discovery II*, commemorating the bicentennial of the Lewis and Clark expedition made one of its earliest stops at Poplar Forest. The exhibit included a high-tech trailer that anchored a huge tent in which performances and discussions explored the many facets of the mission ordered by Jefferson.

From the Collections of Thomas Jefferson's Poplar Forest. Photograph by Octavia N. Starbuck.

He spoke several Indian languages and French. His sixteen-year-old Shoshoni wife Sacagawea (sometimes called "Bird Woman") had previously given birth to an infant son who was two months old by the time she and her husband left Fort Mandan to join Lewis and Clark and their crew on the expedition. Much of the time during the journey she carried the child in a papoose cradle strapped to her back. History records that the young Shoshoni woman was a valuable addition to the crew with her intelligence and knowledge of Indian ways, and as a guide through parts of unknown and potentially dangerous territory.

Then and now, history gives much of the credit for the Louisiana Purchase and the incredible success of the Lewis and Clark expedition to Thomas Jefferson. Despite his critics, there is little doubt but that his popularity during this period helped sweep him back into office.

In November of 1804, in a landslide victory, he was re-elected to serve four more years as president of the United States. George

Clinton, former governor of New York was elected vice president to replace Aaron Burr.

During the summer of 1804, before his term as vice president had expired, Burr had shot and killed his longtime enemy Alexander Hamilton, former secretary of the treasury. The duel ended Burr's political career.

Burr escaped after the duel and for three years conspired to establish an independent nation in the west. He was finally arrested on charges of treason, but at the end of the court trial, presided over by Chief Justice John Marshall, Burr was acquitted for lack of sufficient evidence and was set free. The verdict devastated Jefferson and others who were convinced of Burr's guilt, but they had no recourse.

On March 4, 1805, Jefferson repeated the oath of office in the Senate chamber. In concluding his presidential inaugural address he said: *I shall now enter on the duties to which my fellow citizens have called me again, and shall proceed in the spirit of those principles which they have approved.*

In February of that year, Jefferson had rejoiced over the news that Polly (Mary or Maria), his youngest daughter, had given birth to a baby girl. However, the letters that followed were much less cheerful. She had come down with a fever and was very weak. As soon as he could get away, Jefferson hurried to Monticello, where he found Polly dangerously ill.

Doctors tried to save her, but not yet twenty-six years old, she died on April 17, 1804. Besides her husband John Wayles Eppes, she left behind a son, Francis, almost three. Maria's infant child lived only a short time.

Jefferson was distraught. Depression darkened his days as he tried to cope once again with sorrow. The previous year he had written these sentimental words to Polly: *My feelings of love for you and our dear connections...constitute the only real happiness of my life.*

On April 17, 1804, he wrote a brief notation in his *Memorandum Book: This morning between 8 & 9 o'clock my dear daughter, Maria*

In 2003, Poplar Forest hosted the nationally touring exhibit commemorating the bicentennial of the Lewis and Clark expedition. The tour, dubbed *Corps of Discovery II*, included a tent with an exhibit on the Native American tribes that the expedition met as part of its mission.

From the Collections of Thomas Jefferson's Poplar Forest. Photograph by Octavia N. Starbuck.

Eppes died. Of the six children his wife Martha had borne in the ten years of their marriage, only his daughter Martha remained.

Still grieving over his youngest daughter's death, Jefferson returned to Washington. His involvement with a rash of prickly problems that erupted during his second-term undoubtedly helped distract him from his personal misery.

In the meantime, in the autumn of 1806, Jefferson was cheered by a momentous event. A rider from the U.S. postal station at Cahokia, Illinois, delivered a letter to him in Washington. It was from Captain Meriwether Lewis who reported the safe arrival back of both captains and the Corps of Discovery crew. During their more than 7,000 mile journey through uncharted wilderness, they had explored the Missouri, crossed the Rockies, paddled down the Columbia, reached the Pacific Ocean and *discovered the most practical route which does exist across the country.*

Jefferson read the good news with "unspeakable joy." The adventurers had been gone two years and four months. Lewis promised to give a full account of the expedition during a visit to Washington in December. As part of his message to Congress on December 2, 1806, Jefferson applauded and praised Lewis and Clark for their successful exploration, and announced that they *had learned the character of the country, of its commerce, and inhabitants; and it is but justice to say that Messrs. Lewis and Clarke, and their brave companions, have by their arduous service deserved well of their country.*

They had also fulfilled a great number of Jefferson's requests for Indian artifacts and vocabularies, mineral and botanical species, and many other articles native to western territory. He had received the shipment from the captains more than a year before their actual return.

In 1805, the Corps of Discovery crew had wintered in Fort Mandan. Before setting out on the most dangerous part of the journey through unmapped, unknown territory, Lewis and Clark had shown remarkable foresight. They oversaw the packing of the keelboat with a wide assortment of miscellaneous artifacts and other "treasures" and ordered the crew to return as swiftly as possible to St. Louis. From there the shipment was to be sent to President Thomas Jefferson in Washington.

According to Clark's April 3, 1805 written list of items included in the keelboat's cargo were letters, copies of Lewis and Clark's journals, scientific and geographical reports, maps, Indian artifacts and vocabularies, and hundreds of mineral, botanical and animal specimens. More specifically, according to Clark, the shipment included quantities of animal skins, buffalo and other robes, mountain goat horns, an ear of Mandan Corn, at least one Mandan earthen pot, medicinal roots, seeds, a tin box of insects, bones, and even cages that confined such living creatures as a burrowing squirrel, four living magpies, a prairie dog and a sharp-tailed grouse.

When Lewis finally arrived in Washington on December 28, 1806, he and Clark had been gone approximately two and a half years. Clark did not join him on the Washington visit. Instead, he went to Fincastle, Virginia to be with friends, especially Julia Hancock, whom he thought himself to be in love with, and a girl he meant to court without further delay.

The visit with Jefferson was a time of triumph, of story telling about the journey and displaying additional artifacts he had brought with him to add to those sent to Washington in the 1805 shipment. These included Indian pottery, an Indian "medicine bundle," amulets and examples of handiwork given them by friendly natives, or acquired in trade. He had also persuaded a Mandan chief, Big White, to leave western territory and accompany him to Washington to visit the President "and receive gifts from his own hands." The chief brought along an entourage that included his wife and child. The Mandans joined in some of the celebrations held in honor of Lewis but in time, the natives returned to their tribal lives in the west.

Jefferson was especially pleased with the carefully drawn maps and charts of the western territory that Lewis and Clark had prepared during their travels. He was equally gratified with the contents of their diaries and journals. Altogether, the captains described over 122 animals and reptiles formerly unknown to science and approximately 175 new species of flora and fauna. During the journey, Clark had sketched some of the plants and animals, the people, and various "curiosities." In addition, the men had collected data on 40 different Indian tribes that, as Jefferson had requested, included their native customs, dress, foods, religions, populations, ceremonies, languages and medicine.

The information brought back by Lewis and Clark from their exploration of the new Western Territory increased Jefferson's lifelong interest in Indians. In his second inaugural address, he had expressed his feelings about Native Americans: *Our system is to live in perpetual peace with the Indians, giving them effectual protection against wrongs from our own people.*

In the long philosophic part of his address, Jefferson stated some realistic truths about the future of the tribes and their sur-

vival. He admitted that *a relentless stream of overflowing white population was now overwhelming Indians, and that his administration had
already taken steps to save the Indians from possible extinction.*

Humanity enjoins us to teach them agriculture and the domestic arts,
he said, *to encourage them to that industry which alone can enable them
to maintain their place in existence, and to prepare them in time for that
state of society, which to bodily comforts adds the improvement of mind
and morals.* In other words, he was encouraging the "civilizing" of
the tribes in ways that would force them to change, adapt, and
relinquish their old way of life.

Tragically, for decades, successions of American officials have
continued to force the tribes to surrender their ancestral lands to
whites for colonization and found ways to make them more and
more dependent on the Washington government. Dishonest and
broken treaties ended in betrayal and war. White man's diseases
have caused mass deaths, and the continued enforcement of laws
designed to "civilize" the tribes, destroyed forever the cultures,
traditions, religions, and freedoms of countless Native Americans.

During his long years in public service, Jefferson had stayed in
touch with his plantation overseers at Poplar Forest through letters, and for his own satisfaction, had recorded details of its agricultural activities in his *Farm Book* and other journals.

On September 29, 1805, Jefferson wrote in his *Memorandum
Book* that he had asked Hugh Chisolm, his trusted Irish bricklayer
and carpenter at Monticello, to go to Poplar Forest to begin to
make preparations for building the retreat house he had so often
thought about but delayed beginning. By "preparations," Jefferson
would have meant such tasks as clearing, digging clay for the bricks,
and obtaining sand for mortar, gathering stones, leveling the
ground, and excavating for the foundation.

During the following months, Chisolm wrote letters to Washington giving progress reports on the work at Bedford. Jefferson,
who once described his employee as "a very good humored man,"
must have had complete trust in Chisolm's ability to get the job
done, as well as in the bricklayer's integrity, dependability, loyalty,
and optimism in regard to the project.

Poplar Forest hosted the nationally touring *Corps of Discovery II* exhibit in honor of Jefferson's role in authoring the Lewis and Clark expedition. The exhibit allowed visitors to journey along the Lewis and Clark trail, introducing them to the Native Americans, geography, wildlife and botany that Lewis and Clark painstakingly recorded.

From the Collections of Thomas Jefferson's Poplar Forest.   Photograph by Octavia N. Starbuck.

The duties of the presidency and other demands kept Jefferson from going to Bedford for almost nine months after Chisolm went to Bedford. Finally, in a June 16, 1806 letter to Martha, Jefferson wrote: *I find by a letter from Chisolm that I shall have to proceed to Bedford almost without stopping in Albemarle. I shall probably be kept there a week or 10 days laying the foundation of the house, which he is not equal to himself, so that it will be near the middle of August before I shall be fixed at Monticello.*

His young grandson Thomas Jefferson Randolph (Jeff for short), almost fourteen, went with him on the journey to Poplar Forest. Once the foundation was laid with bricks and rocks, the next step was the actual construction. Between 1789 and 1794, Jefferson had begun to draw designs for constructing a building on a high point of land for what appears to have been a villa. Prior to making a decision on the style of the house, he apparently considered several alternative designs, including one made around 1804 labeled "Plan for Bedford."

The architectural style he finally chose for the Poplar Forest property was octagonal in shape. Each of the rooms would be elongated, octagonal in structure, designed to admit a free flow of air and light. The exception was the center room (to serve as the dining room) that would form a perfect cube, with the ceiling height and four walls each measuring twenty feet. An over-sixteen foot long skylight was centered overhead.

In planning his retreat, Jefferson chose the Tuscan order, the simplest design of all the ancient Roman orders, for the columns and to form the proportions of the exterior of Poplar Forest. Jefferson did not pretend that he was a professionally trained architect. He gained most of his knowledge from diverse reading on architecture, from observation, from the sound classical education he had received at William and Mary and his own natural bent for building and desire to create beauty.

His preference for classical Roman architecture for its precision, order, balance and simplicity had not changed since his student days, nor after he had designed and supervised the construction and remodeling of Monticello He remembered his five years in France and his admiration for buildings in the neoclassical style. He also re-read and referred to *Four Books of Architecture* by the Italian master designer Andrea Palladio whose principles of architecture were also advocated by the first century B.C. Roman architect Vitruvius. Both men believed that natural forms led to superior architectural orders that had been tested for centuries and had an objective form of beauty.

Other books that influenced Jefferson in planning his Bedford retreat were from the English Palladian movement. The most important of these were architectural works written by William Kent (1727), Robert Morris (1755), and James Gibbs (1728). It is little wonder then that Jefferson's master plan for his Poplar Forest house and the surrounding landscape were based on the classical form of architecture, but also included some features that reflected his own imagination, knowledge and personal taste.

Early reconstruction underway at Poplar Forest.

Photograph by the author.

Poplar Forest Floor Plan

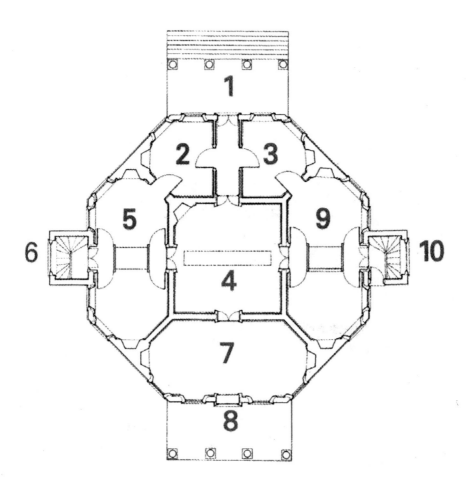

Key to the Floor Plan

1. **North Portico**
2. **Northwest Room**
    Storage/Spare Bedroom
3. **Northeast Room**
    Storage/Spare Bedroom
4. **Dining Room**
5. **West Bedroom**
    Jefferson's Bedroom
6. **West Stair Pavilion**
7. **Parlor (South Room)**
8. **South Portico**
9. **East Bedroom**
    Grandchildren's Bedroom
10. **East Stair Pavilion**

Programs continue throughout the restoration of Jefferson's Poplar Forest.

Photograph by the author.

CHAPTER 6

A RETREAT HOME AND RETIREMENT

It (house at Poplar Forest) is an Octagon of 50 f. diameter, of brick, well built, will be plaistered this fall, when nothing will be wanting to finish it compleatly but the cornices and some of the doors. When finished, it will be the best dwelling house in the state, except that of Monticello; perhaps preferable to that, as more proportioned to the faculties of a private citizen.

Thomas Jefferson to John Wayles Eppes, 1812

During the final years of Jefferson's presidency, he corresponded with his workmen in Bedford County through letters regarding miscellaneous construction problems at his Poplar Forest house. Sometimes their replies contained progress reports.

One of the most interesting of these reports was written by Hugh Chisolm, dated June 1, 1807, in which he informed Jefferson that *the walls are all leveal except the squar room.* He indicated that he and the other workmen were making good progress and mentioned that he was *now ready for the window and door frames,* which, incidentally, were being made at Monticello.

Jefferson replied promptly, giving Chisolm further instructions about the doors and window frames. In a postscript he added:

If you would engage the negroes to dig and remove the earth South of the house, 90 feet wide down to a foot below the lower floor, and descending from thence due south 1 inch in every 10 ft. till it gets clear out of the ground, I would gladly pay them for it." He also said that the slaves who undertook the digging project should do so *only with their own free will and undertaking to do it in their own time.*

In other words, Jefferson was asking Chisolm to oversee the digging of a sunken lawn to extend south of the house similar to the sunken lawns or terraces he had seen in his travels abroad. Other landscaping projects that he was to introduce in later years were all part of his instructions for *planting and improving the grounds.*

Jefferson traveled to Bedford County in early September of 1807, for what turned out to be a short visit. He was undoubtedly pleased to see that, as he had requested in his letter, one of his slaves Phil Hubbard and an uncertain number of helpers had been digging the sunken lawn south of the house. Though not yet finished, day by day the workers hauled the dirt fill in wheelbarrows to locations east and west of the excavation to form two ornamental mounds that grew higher and higher.

As for the house itself, Jefferson found that his workmen had made good progress. They used timbers from the surrounding forests and from his holdings in Albemarle, to construct doors, window frames, floors and on and on. There was almost constant travel between Poplar Forest and Monticello. The procession included slaves who alternated working at Poplar Forest and Monticello and a caravan of wagons carrying building materials and other cargo.

After Jefferson's return home to Monticello, his future retreat must have remained much in his thoughts—so much so that he began planning for the inside furnishings. Before he went back to Washington that fall, he wrote to George Jefferson who was an agent of Jefferson's in Richmond requesting that the three dozen "stick" or Windsor chairs he had ordered be sent by boat to Lynchburg. He also arranged with a Richmond firm to ship by

The sunken south lawn is one of the remaining features of Jefferson's original landscape scheme. Archaeologists excavated the lawn's banks and temporarily ornamented them with plants to learn more about Jefferson's design.

From the Collections of Thomas Jefferson's Poplar Forest

boat *some crockery ware for my use in Bedford* to be taken *by stage conveyance* and thence to Lynchburg.

Jefferson was undoubtedly pleased by a piece of good news written by Hugh Chisolm in an 1807 letter in regard to progress being made on the construction in the west bedroom. *If it be possible for to get a room finished for you agin the time you told me you wood come to see us it shall be certenly done and I think if I go on uninterruptly I shall have it ready.* In a later letter, he had been even more encouraging: *Mr. Perry has laid the flow {floor} in west room and is now studing the alcove, as soon as he is done that I shall bricknog and plaster it for your reception.*

Through the years, Jefferson depended on a number of skilled carpenters who worked at both Monticello and Poplar Forest. Among these were John and Reuben Perry, and John Hemings, a slave with exceptional ability as a carpenter and joiner who did much of the finish work on the house.

On January 8, 1808, James Dinsmore, another of Jefferson's best carpenters and builders at Monticello, wrote to his employer saying, *We must make the sashes for P. Forest as soon as it is dry,* and was concerned that *there has not been any glass got, for the Bedford sashes.*

When Jefferson replied to Dinsmore's letter, he had disappointing news. The glass for the Poplar Forest window sashes that he had ordered from Philadelphia could not be shipped until spring when the ice thawed on the Delaware River. It was mid-March before Jefferson again wrote to Dinsmore to report that the eight boxes of glass that had been sent from Washington to Alexandria *were to be forwarded by the first vessel to Richmond.*

The nails used by the carpenters in building Poplar Forest were made in Jefferson's nailery that was housed in his blacksmith shop along Mulberry Row, a 1,000-foot-long road at Monticello where the slaves worked in shops at various small industries, or in mild weather, outside in the yards. They cut and shaped nails on forges from iron rods, with the help of anvils and hammers. Nailboys, most of them young male slaves aged ten to sixteen, made certain strikes and movements to form nails of different lengths and diameters. An overseer probably inspected the finished nails.

The nailery industry served its purpose. Large quantities of nails were needed for Jefferson's ongoing building projects at Monticello as well as at Poplar Forest. In addition, merchants in the surrounding counties often purchased supplies of nails from Jefferson. Some nails at that time were cut and formed by a machine, but most of those made at Monticello were hand-wrought. Jefferson's *Account Book* showed a small profit from the nailery during the early years, but later on, for whatever reasons, it no longer succeeded as a profitable operation.

Hugh Chisolm had written to Jefferson in February of 1808, about the brick-making prospects at Poplar Forest, explaining that preparations were delayed because of his work at Monticello. However, he assured his employer that the *earth had been turned up the second time for the bricks* and that his brother John *would now prepare the yard to lay them on* and help produce quantities of bricks. According to notes Chisolm made later that year, his brother started work at Poplar Forest on March 10.

Before Chisolm had begun to make bricks for laying the foundation for the house he had wisely selected a suitable site for brick making. He knew that the best location would be as close to the construction site as possible, and near water where quantities of sand and good clay were readily available.

Generally, the fall of the year was the best time for such work. The clay had to be dug, cleared of stone, and after sand was added, soaked in pits, and allowed to weather over the winter. On milder days, workmen blended the mixture by trampling it underfoot, using either animals or bare human feet.

Under Hugh Chisolm's direction, the workmen made special molds to shape curved bricks, pre-shaped for the bases of columns that support the north and south porticos. They also devised special molds to produce bricks that could be used to form the walls for Jefferson's octagonal house. They are called squint (or pentagonal) bricks and are similar to ordinary bricks except for the special angles at one end that make them five-sided. Sometimes broken or misshapen squint bricks that were called "wasters" served other purposes, such as in the case of Poplar Forest, many were used to lay the floor for the wine cellar on the lower level.

After the spring thaw, workmen would pour the brick mixture into wooden forms, let the bricks air-dry for a week or more, then stack and fire them in one or more hardwood-burning kilns for five days.

In a letter Chisolm wrote to Jefferson in July of that same year (1808), he was obviously proud of the success of the brick-making project. *It is my wish to inform you, how we are coming on with our work at this place,* he wrote. *We have burnt the bricks, and a finer kiln I never burnt in my life, it contains seventy five thousand. . . .* The kiln was fired three times in order to produce 240,000 bricks.

In another letter, written to his employer that September, Chisolm referred to still another project—the construction of two matching "necessaries" (privies) located on either side of the mounds, east and west. He wrote that he had already finished *one of the necessaries, and in the course of this week I will have the other done.* After helping to lay the foundation for Jefferson's octagonal house,

Hugh Chisolm probably experienced little or no difficulty in using the same design.

Meanwhile back in Washington, Jefferson was surrounded by turmoil. His most worrisome political problem was the war that continued to rage between England and France and the danger of America becoming involved. His decision to stay neutral and try to keep the country at peace, resulted in sharp criticism by many members of Congress (including certain of his supporters) of his handling of foreign relations. Businessmen, shippers, traders, and ordinary citizens joined in the insistent demand that he abandon his policy of neutrality.

After the failure of attempted negotiations with the British, Jefferson realized that the Congress would either have to declare war or pass a bill recommending that an embargo be placed on all foreign trade. He reminded Congress that American vessels and seamen *were continually threatened on the high seas and elsewhere, from the belligerent powers of Europe.* In 1807, Congress approved Jefferson's proposal for an Embargo Act that forbade the departure of vessels from American ports.

Opponents of the act feared that cutting off all foreign shipping would hurt the American economy more than it would create hardships in England and France. The embargo and Jefferson's policy of neutrality began with moderate public support, but as the weeks passed, both he and the Embargo Act met with intense disapproval and opposition. Confused and worried, Jefferson knew he had to make a decision. He finally admitted that to continue to defend his foreign no-trade policy was useless and conceded that *war will become preferable to continuance of the embargo after a certain time.*

Over a year before, he had confessed to his good friend James Monroe that *longings for retirement are so strong, that I with difficulty encounter the daily drudgeries of my duty.* He was discouraged with his role as president and, during his final months in office, felt that he had failed the American people. The vicious personal and political criticism that had marked his second term continued to sting his sensitive nature. Though he forced himself to carry out the most pressing needs of his office, he began to pack his belongings in preparation for his long-anticipated return to Monticello.

Jefferson was pleased when his friend James Madison was elected the fourth President of the United States. As the day of Madison's inauguration neared he wrote to a friend: *Within a few days I retire to my family, my books, and farms...Never did a prisoner released from his chains feel such relief as I shall on shaking off the shackles of power.*

Jefferson stood alongside Madison during the administration of the oath of office, but refused to participate in any of the public ceremonies or to draw attention to himself and away from the new President. Despite urging by officials, he even declined an invitation to sit near Madison in the Hall of Representatives. *This day I return to the people,* he said quietly, *and my proper seat is among them.*

Following the inauguration ceremonies he slipped away on his horse as unobtrusively as possible. Back in his rooms, he continued packing his books and other personal belongings. Among these were the scientific specimens and other articles from the successful Lewis and Clark expedition, along with records of the 1807 explorations of Zebulon Pike who, at Jefferson's request, had also explored western lands, adding greatly to the existing scientific and geographical data.

On March 11, 1809, after nearly a week of final preparations and farewells to the Madison family, friends and colleagues, Jefferson set out for Virginia. This time he knew that he was leaving Washington behind forever and that he would never again return to politics or government service. Free at last, he would spend his remaining years at Monticello and at Poplar Forest, which was soon to become his beloved getaway retreat.

Jefferson's remark concerning his relief at leaving behind the "shackles of power" was not overstated, and his delight in the pleasures of domestic life and being with his family did not lessen during the years to come. At the same time, he did not neglect his own personal interests and pursuits. When at Poplar Forest, he tried to arrange each day so that he could accomplish as much as possible. To him, reading, writing, thinking and architecture, his various scientific pursuits, and his gardens and orchards were of prime importance.

He wrote in a letter to a friend, *the total change of occupation from the house and writing table to constant employment in the garden and farm has added wonderfully to my happiness.*

In addition to his main money crops of tobacco and wheat, Jefferson the agronomist, tried to produce more and better species of fruits and vegetables and maintain valuable nutrients in the soil. Though he continued to rely on old favorites such as pumpkins, red beets, carrots, peas, millet, hemp, flax, and other such familiar crops on his plantation, he also experimented with grafting trees and bushes and introducing new plants and seeds into Virginia's red clay soil.

Some years before, he had drawn up a list of his most important accomplishments. On the list, Jefferson had included the sending of olive trees and upland rice to South Carolina, along with the drafting of the Declaration of Independence, the act for religious freedom, and the act for the diffusion of knowledge. He was so convinced of the importance of agriculture to mankind that he had once commented that *the greatest service which can be rendered any country is to add a useful plant to its culture.*

After his retirement, Jefferson's optimistic plan was to live off his income from farming, particularly at Poplar Forest. He hoped to erase his debts that, at the time, amounted to approximately $11,000. Sadly, this hope was not to be realized.

By the time Jefferson left Washington to return to Virginia in March of 1809, the basic construction work on his Poplar Forest retreat had been completed. At the same time, a great deal remained to be done. The walls were up but not plastered; the roof was sheathed, but not yet overlaid with chestnut shingles; and though some of the oak floors were laid, they were far from finished. Doors had to be hung; the balustrade railing had to be installed as part of the roof; and the list of other unfinished jobs went on.

It was November of that year before Jefferson found time to visit his new house. After arriving, he found that Hugh Chisolm, his dependable "man of all trades," had kept his promise. The alcove in the west bedroom was sufficiently finished for him to sleep in his own bed in his own private sleeping quarters.

An alcove is a recess within a room for a bed. *Chambre al alcove* is French in origin and was probably introduced into this country by Jefferson. Monticello has examples of alcoves both against a wall and in the middle of a room with a space on both sides, as in Jefferson's bedroom at his retreat. A similar alcove bed was installed in the east bedroom at Poplar Forest that would become the sleeping quarters for some of his grandchildren.

After Jefferson's 1809 visit, he began making trips to Poplar Forest three or four times a year, usually staying a week or longer, sometimes a month or more. He did not confine his visits there to any one season. Dates on letters written at Poplar Forest, show that he traveled to his retreat at different periods of the year, sometimes even in winter, but for practical reasons he tried to schedule visits to coincide with spring planting, the cultivation of crops in summer and the fall harvest. Each time while in residence, he helped oversee the farm operations and suggested ways to increase production.

At age 66, Jefferson's hair was almost white, but he was still slender and stood straight and tall. Periodically, attacks of rheumatism continued to slow his physical activities, but at other times he insisted on following a fairly rigorous schedule. Unfortunately, the ailment could flare up unexpectedly. During one summer trip to his Poplar Forest plantation he had confessed in a letter to William Burwell, written after his arrival, that he had *suffered much coming, staying and shall returning.*

However, despite the discomfort, he continued to make the long three-day trips to Bedford County, knowing that when he arrived at his country villa, he would enjoy the leisure, solitude, and quiet that always awaited him.

When Jefferson was at Poplar Forest, he followed a daily routine similar to the one he kept at Monticello in the years after leaving public office. He got up at sunrise, soaked his feet in cold water, ate an early breakfast, then rode around his property, both to check on his slaves and the farming activities, and, one can assume, for exercise and enjoyment.

Jefferson had dinner at 3 or 4 o'clock, and then retired for several hours until late afternoon when he spent time with family members, if any had accompanied him to Poplar Forest. After tea was served, Jefferson would read. Tallow and whale sperm oil were used for candles, and in time, myrtle wax. He usually went to bed around 10 o'clock.

During his sometimes-lengthy stays at his retreat, another of his occupations was corresponding with relatives, former government allies, and friends during mornings spent in the south room (or parlor). In 1810, he had advised his grandson Jeff Randolph by mail to *write a letter to somebody every morning...As most of the business of life, and all our friendly communications are by way of letter, nothing is more important than to acquire a facility of developing our ideas on paper.*

During the day, he allowed himself time for leisure and to attend to farm activities. The labor of cultivating tobacco alone was a yearly challenge that demanded much of the enslaved population of workers at Poplar Forest, beginning with the planting in Spring and the continuing cultivation through the long hot summer. A successful crop required such endless work as weeding, transplanting, hoeing, suckering and finally, taking the crop to drying barns located at various points on the property. When the leaves were properly cured, slaves collected all the tobacco at what was called the prize barn, where they pressed the leaves into large barrels called hogsheads with a lever known as a prize. Jefferson, or his current overseer, then arranged for the sale and transport of the tobacco to Lynchburg, and thence to Richmond or other markets down the James River in flat-bottomed boats called bateaux.

Busy days notwithstanding, Jefferson tried to find time to work in his vegetable garden for his own pleasure, to supervise the continuing work on his house, and to oversee the planting

The James River between Lynchburg and Richmond formed a crucial commercial water route that Jefferson used to transport crops from his Poplar Forest plantation. Every spring Virginians re-create the historic journeys of the flat-bottomed boats called bateaux.

Photograph by the author

of additional trees, flowers, shrubs and other plantings that would enhance his ornamental landscape.

In a letter written at Poplar Forest in 1811, to his friend Charles Willson Peale, Jefferson praised the special delights of horticulture: *I have often thought that if heaven had given me choice of my position and calling, it should have been on a rich spot of earth, well watered and near a good market for the productions of the garden. No occupation is so delightful to me as the culture of the earth and no culture comparable to that of the garden. Such a variety of subjects, some are always coming to perfection, the failure of one thing repaired by the success of another, and instead of one harvest, a continued one through the year. Under total want of demand, except for our family table I am still devoted to the garden, but tho an old man, I am but a young gardener.*

Poplar Forest with the original Jefferson design features restored.
From the Collections of Thomas Jefferson's Poplar Forest.

CHAPTER 7

LIFE AT POPLAR FOREST

I write to you from a place, 90 miles from Monticello, near the New London of this state, which I visit three or four times a year. I stay from a fortnight to a month at a time. I have fixed myself comfortably, keep some books here, bring others occasionally, am in the solitude of a hermit, and quite at leisure to attend to my absent friends...I find friendship to be like wine, raw when new, ripened with age, the true old man's milk and restorative cordial.

From a letter written by Thomas Jefferson at Poplar Forest to Benjamin Rush (a well-known Philadelphia doctor and fellow signer of the *Declaration of Independence*), August 1811.

Soon after returning to Monticello from a trip to Poplar Forest in December of 1810 where he spent Christmas, Jefferson wrote to John Barnes, a long-time business acquaintance and friend in Georgetown, giving an account of his well-being: *I continue in the enjoyment of good health, take much exercise and make frequent journeys to Bedford the only journeys I now take, or ever expect to take.*

Jefferson's remark to his friend was not entirely accurate in light of the future trips the former president was to undertake within

Virginia, but after 1810 he did try to confine more of his travels to going back and forth between his two homes.

Taking a chance on the weather, Jefferson traveled to Poplar Forest in late January 1811. He was concerned about his wheat crop in Bedford that had to be milled into flour and shipped to Richmond for sale. Not having a mill at Poplar Forest, he must have the work done elsewhere, but a recent flood had breached the dam at his favorite mill and he was obliged to find another to do the grinding.

Jefferson was still in Bedford on February 24 when he wrote to his daughter Martha, complaining with some bitterness about the frustrating weather:

The weather has been such that I have seen the face of no human beings for days but the servants. I am like a state prisoner. My keepers set before me at fixed hours something to eat and withdraw. We have had seven snows since I came, making all together about 10 ½ inches. The ground has been now covered a fortnight. I had begun to prepare an Asparagus bed, and to plant some raspberry bushes, gooseberry bushes, etc. for Anne (his oldest granddaughter), *but it has been impossible to go on with it, the earth is so deep frozen, and I expect to leave it so.*

On each mound he planted weeping willows, golden willows and aspens, three of his favorite trees. He also had a special fondness for paper mulberries and for aspens, redbuds, dogwoods, and poplars—Athenian, Lombardy and Balsam. His idea of good landscape design was to intermingle not just trees, but when possible, a variety of shrubs, such as calycanthus, lilacs, and roses, with annual and perennial flowers of every description.

When Jefferson made his third trip to Poplar Forest in 1811, his grandson Jeff Randolph, went along again for company. Soon after their arrival, Jefferson took time to write a long memorandum to Jeremiah Goodman, his newest overseer, to help acquaint him with his farm duties, what crops were to be planted in which fields, and the general working of the plantation. He also listed many of the names of the slave families on the place, along with their assigned tasks and special skills.

In the memorandum he mentioned Hanah, *who cooks & washes for me when I am here,* and Bess, who he mentioned divided her time between the dairy and her own home but who *makes the butter during the season, to be sent to Monticello in the winter.* Jefferson asked Goodman *to give special attention to Nace, the former headman, and the best we have ever known, [who] is to be entirely kept from labour until he recovers, which will probably be long. He may do anything which he can do sitting in a warm room, such as shoemaking and making baskets. He can shell corn in the corn house when it is quite warm, or in his own house at anytime.*

The memo further stated that should any of the slaves become ill, *let our neighbor Dr. Steptoe be called in.* Dr. William Steptoe was a neighborhood doctor who became one of Jefferson's good friends. Letters and other sources substantiate the fact that if Jefferson was present when one or more slaves took sick, he sometimes relied on his own knowledge of medicine. He believed that illnesses should not be treated with harsh practices such as bleeding and purging but "with a lighter diet and kind attention."

Considering Jefferson's wide reading in anatomy and medicine, it can be safely said that he was more knowledgeable about healing simple physical problems than some of the doctors of his era, who often had no medical education or degrees but practiced it as a trade. At Monticello, and later at Poplar Forest, he looked after the physical care of the slaves. He learned how to set bones, apply stitches to open wounds, and lance an abscess. To his credit, he kept a supply of Jenner's smallpox vaccine on hand that he had obtained in Boston to vaccinate his slaves as protection against the dreaded plague.

Jefferson publicly admitted more than once that the practice of keeping other human beings in bondage was wrong and *a moral and political depravity,* but he, like most other Virginia landowners, depended on slaves to cultivate the land and to do other farm labor.

To his credit, he had tried several times to end the slave trade from Africa. One instance occurred at the first session of the Virginia assembly after independence when he had encouraged and supported a law prohibiting the importation of slaves that, he believed, would halt the *increases of this great political and moral evil.* The bill had not passed. Later in his life he admitted that he did not know how to solve the problems of slavery, but during his presidency he argued for the abolition of the slave trade. Congress passed a law prohibiting the trade in 1808 but it was widely ignored.

Seven enslaved families lived at Poplar Forest by the 1790s. Four generations of a single family were on the property when Jefferson died in 1826. When children were ten years old, or younger, they looked after younger brothers and sisters while their parents worked in the fields or at other tasks. Sometimes older children helped to plant seeds and weed or assisted in other less strenuous tasks. When young men and women reached age sixteen they became part of the plantation work force.

Adults, both the weaker slaves and those who were strong and healthy, usually worked from early morning until evening, six days a week. On Sundays, they were free from plantation tasks. They could visit New London or go elsewhere, tend their own private gardens, and enjoy being with their families. Close networks of communication with kinfolk reached beyond Poplar Forest to Jefferson's other plantations.

Research into Jefferson's treatment of his slaves indicates that he probably tried to be fair and, in fact, considered them part of his extended family. In turn, a few who learned to read and write are known to have written letters to him expressing respect and affection. He occasionally paid cash to anyone who labored overtime beyond a usual day's work, or for purchases of chickens and turkeys. In some circumstances, however, Jefferson sanctioned the use of harsh punishments and he sometimes sold slaves. Though he generally disapproved of cruel physical treatment, during his absences some of his overseers whipped and otherwise mistreated some of the slaves.

Although he did appear to try to keep families together, he did not always do so. Among other instances, records tell us that Jefferson sold forty Poplar Forest slaves in Bedford County during the 1790s. Individual slaves he considered to be troublesome, and those who repeatedly ran away, would in all likelihood have been among the first to be sold.

Like most plantation owners, Jefferson made efforts to make his farm communities as self-sufficient as possible. At least partial independence of the outside world was especially necessary at a plantation such as Poplar Forest where stores and other sources of supplies were limited and somewhat scattered.

As a consequence, he was responsible for the overall care of his slaves. He had to provide food, shelter and clothing for every man, woman and child, whether able to work or not. Of course, even in lean harvests, the slaves helped supplement the rations allotted them by the farm overseer; they grew or gathered fruits and vegetables, preserved, hunted, fished, and raised poultry for meat and eggs to add variety to their diets.

Providing sets of winter and summer clothing, blankets, and beds for each slave was expensive and worrisome, especially when cloth grew scarce and, at times, disappeared entirely from merchants' shelves. Shortages occurred when shipping restrictions were put on imported goods from Britain during the War of 1812. Another cause was poor harvests, the sad aftermath of droughts, hail storms, or other adverse weather conditions. Sometimes, when plantation weavers failed to turn out enough homespun, or lacked enough cloth for other reasons, Jefferson had to purchase supplies to keep everyone adequately clothed. As the war intensified even further, he responded to the crisis by putting even more emphasis on the cottage industries of spinning and weaving at his plantations.

On February 12, 1812, Jefferson wrote Goodman, then his overseer, expressing the hope that *the spinning and weaving has got well under way.* During this period Jefferson set up spinning and weaving operations at both Poplar Forest and Monticello. He informed his overseer that his efforts to buy cotton or oznaburg in Richmond had not been successful and that there was no chance of *clothing the negroes next winter but with what we shall make ourselves.* Later, he instructed Goodman to send Sally and Maria [to

Monticello] to learn to weave & spin but, when she returned to Poplar Forest, Sally had to be replaced by a girl with more natural ability. Other spinners at the time included Bess, Lucy, Abby, Nisy, and Cate.

At Poplar Forest, Jefferson already had an early form of spinning machine called a spinning jenny, which he described as *a very fine one with 12 spindles,* but he saw the need for a larger machine. He wrote to his overseer Jeremiah Goodwin, telling him to make the door of the spinning house *4f6i, wide in the clear to let in the machine of 24 spindles.* The spinning house in Bedford was ready for use in 1813.

Jefferson also gave instructions to his overseer regarding which female slaves were to spin not only wool, but also cotton and flax, and which were to be weavers. Servants, trained as weavers on his plantations, turned out goodly quantities of cloth from yarn or thread, using looms with flying shuttles. Most looms were so big and bulky that weavers worked at their craft in outbuildings.

In Jefferson's day, much of the raw materials for making cloth were grown or raised on farms or plantations, and Poplar Forest was no exception. Experienced spinners and weavers knew that a blend of different fibers, usually linen, cotton and wool, made fabric more durable and longwearing.

It is unlikely that Jefferson would have tried to raise cotton because of the climate in Bedford County but it was raised for certain in warmer parts of the south and shipped by boat to fill orders elsewhere. Growing and harvesting the crop demanded hard work, but with the invention of the cotton gin in 1793 by Eli Whitney, farmers increased production. A gin could do the work of a hundred slaves so that, in time, prices dropped until it was cheaper than linen and in great demand.

The planting and growing of small amounts of flax to make linen for plantation use was one of Jefferson's crops at Poplar Forest. It grew readily in Virginia soil, and was useful in keeping workers in the enslaved community adequately clothed.

As part of the preparation for use, the stalks had to be soaked first in water, perhaps a millpond, or deep stream. Afterwards, the plant stalks were crushed in wooden devices called brakes, to remove bark and other debris from the fibers before they could be spun into thread.

Another important fabric was, of course, the wool sheared from the sheep raised at Poplar Forest. For warmth, there was no substitute—for blankets, clothes, and other cold-weather needs. Around 1809, Jefferson had decided to raise and breed his own sheep at Poplar Forest. He especially prized his Spanish Merinos, a breed that he thought produced superior wool. In fact, he was so enthusiastic about Merinos that he described them as a "valuable race" and encouraged other landowners to raise and breed them on Virginia farms.

Before sheep's wool could be used, it had to be thoroughly washed and cleaned. This process required several steps. After the scouring, or washing, the fibers had to be handpicked free of burrs, seeds, fragments of bark and other unwanted material. Next came the carding, which was done primarily to straighten and separate the wool fibers in preparation for spinning. This part of the process was done with two special paddles, or cards, that had sharp wire surfaces. Finally, the rolls of wool, known as rolags, became soft and fluffy enough to be twisted into yarn and made ready for weaving.

Women did much of the work necessary to produce sufficient quantities of fabric to be made into clothes for all seasons, including the spinning and weaving. In addition to endless household and other chores they worked in the fields during the growing season and helped bring in the harvest. Though Jefferson differentiated between types of fieldwork assigned to men and women, regardless of gender, both labored at farming on a regular basis.

Men had their own tasks to complete. At Poplar Forest, as at Monticello, blacksmiths shod horses, made tools, wrought iron implements and utensils. Other workers, called coopers, used wooden staves to make buckets and barrels for storage, shipping and other uses. Still others were trained as carpenters.

Jefferson continued to employ approximately fifty to seventy-five enslaved workers (sometimes as many as one hundred) in

Bedford County. Growing and harvesting tobacco continued to be the plantation's main money crop, both as an export and a medium of exchange.

In addition to the hard work demanded of slaves who made tobacco growing possible, it exhausted the soil and produced nothing tangible for their daily good or for that of the landowners. There is no record that Jefferson ever used tobacco personally but grew it for economic survival.

In 1781, during an extended stay at Poplar Forest with his family, he had written a condemnation of tobacco and its growth as *a culture productive of infinite wretchedness. Those employed in it are in a continued state of exertion beyond the powers of nature to support.*

Because tobacco culture on his plantations did not always provide a reliable source of income, at intervals Jefferson tried to substitute other crops. In later years at Poplar Forest, he came to depend more and more on wheat, both as a money crop and as a source of good quality bread flour for daily use.

As Jefferson grew older, his concerns increased over the dwindling prices paid for crops of almost every sort. Many farmers throughout the Piedmont in Virginia shared his uneasiness. For one thing, tobacco had already exhausted the soil in many fields, and the problem of maintaining an adequate number of slaves intensified as incomes dropped due to the low prices paid for produce. Plantation owners frequently encountered one disaster after another. Some were caused by "acts of nature" such as extremes in weather during the growing season. Those like Jefferson, who increasingly turned to wheat as a money crop, were devastated when armadas of "Hessian flies" attacked their fields and destroyed the harvest.

While recovering from a bout of rheumatism during a visit to Poplar Forest in August, 1811, Jefferson spent a good deal of his time writing letters to Benjamin Rush, to Charles Willson Peale, and other friends from his past. His correspondence with other friends and former colleagues such as President James Madison and Secretary of State James Monroe undoubtedly helped keep him from feeling isolated from the outside world, though he had lost interest in politics and no longer tried to keep up with the latest news or happenings in government.

He also enjoyed conversing with and writing to a local Bedford County friend, Rev. Charles Clay. On August 20, 1811, in one of his letter to Clay he wrote: *While here and much confined to the house by my rheumatism, I have amused myself with calculating the hour lines of an horizontal disk for the latitude of this place, which I find to be 37°22'26". The calculations are for every 5 minutes of time and are always exact to within less than half a second of a degree.*

Jefferson's general correspondence included letters to members of his family at Monticello, other relatives and acquaintances. Approximately 20,000 letters, many of them copies, still survive. He may have written far more in his lifetime, but approximately that number have been documented.

He also received many letters in return. *Every mail brings a fresh load,* he once remarked. *They are letters of inquiry for the most part, always of good will, sometimes from friends whom I esteem, but much oftener from persons whose names are unknown to me, but written kindly and civilly, and to which, therefore, civility requires answers.*

A polygraph copying machine Jefferson once called "the finest invention of the present age" was a valuable tool in Jefferson's correspondence, as well as in his general writing. It was one of his most prized possessions at Poplar Forest.

An Englishman, John Isaac Hawkins, who lived for a time in Pennsylvania, had invented the polygraph in 1802. Hawkins described his invention in an advertisement that appeared in *Poulson's American Daily Advertiser.* It read:

> THE POLYGRAPH enables a person to write two or three letters, other writings, or even drawings, at the same instant of time, with equal freedom and ease as is done with a single pen. So obvious is the importance of having exact copies of Letters or other transactions to every man and woman, who ever writes on business or even on the most trivial concerns.

When Hawkins decided to leave Pennsylvania and return to England, Jefferson's friend Charles Willson Peale agreed to act as an agent for Hawkins' invention. Peale was to oversee the manufacturing and marketing of the copy machine in the United States. Enthusiastic about the polygraph, Peale and Jefferson made additional modifications and improvements before advertising it to the public. Jefferson bought one for Monticello and one for the President's House in Washington. The one Jefferson used at Poplar Forest was sent to him from England as a gift by the inventor Hawkins. It is thought to have been a finer instrument than earlier more "primitive" machines.

In December, 1811, the last of Jefferson's visits to Poplar Forest that year, he decided to reconcile by letter with a former close friend and government ally, John Adams, with whom he had developed political differences and misunderstandings. In recent years, the two men had not seen each other or kept in touch by mail.

Benjamin Rush, a friend of both men, knew of their alienation and in his correspondence had encouraged the renewal of their friendship—before it was too late. John Adams had passed his seventy-sixth birthday and suffered from nerve palsy. Jefferson was somewhat younger but not without physical problems.

Doctor Rush decided to act as mediator. He wrote letters to each man—suggesting reconciliation. Jefferson agreed to make the effort but hesitated to take the first step. Then, by chance, he learned of a complimentary statement John Adams had made about him to mutual friends while they were visiting Adams in New England.

"I always loved Jefferson, and still love him." Adams was reported to have said about him during a conversation.

Jefferson was so pleased by the comment that he wrote back to Rush expressing his willingness to make peace with Adams and to settle their differences, saying, *I only needed this knowledge to revive towards him all the affections of the most cordial moments of our lives.*

Soon afterwards, when he received an affectionate letter from John Adams, all former barriers toppled and Jefferson wrote back, saying in part:

Polygraph: Jefferson turned to the best technology of his day, a twin-penned polygraph, to copy all of his correspondence. He brought a traveling version of the machine to Poplar Forest. A reproduction of the polygraph is displayed in the house.

From the Collections of Thomas Jefferson's Poplar Forest. Photograph by Jackie Almond.

A letter from you calls up recollections very dear to my mind. It carries me back to the times when, beset with difficulties and dangers, we were fellow laborers in the same cause, struggling for what is most valuable to man, his right of self-government.

Thereafter, the exchange of letters between the two men marked the beginning of a correspondence that lasted fourteen years. They wrote on a wide variety of subjects. Most of the letters were witty, educational, and rich in history. Although the two men did not always agree, they were careful not to criticize one another or make offensive remarks for fear of destroying their renewed friendship.

Today, scholars and admirers of Jefferson and Adams can still read their correspondence. Many of the letters are affectionate, even sentimental. They provide enduring facts about an important era in our nation's history, and personal insights into the hearts, minds and characters of both.

In addition to correspondence and other forms of writing, reading continued to be of great importance to Jefferson. He had approximately 700 books in his library at Poplar Forest. The collection included his petit-format (very small-sized) books by such authors as Cicero, Virgil, Tacitus, Caesar, Ovid, Horace, Aesop, and Homer. These small volumes were bound in "calf and red morocco" and kept in "4 bookcases with mahogany sashes." Some of the other books in his collection included a 52-volume set of Buffon's *Histoire Naturelle* and Bell's edition of Shakespeare and volumes of Italian and French and a few favorite Greek and Latin books of prose and poetry.

Apparently his reading was not always heavy or of a serious nature as evidenced in a letter he wrote to his friend Elizabeth Trist in May 1813: *I bought the inclosed book to this place [Poplar Forest], the last fall, intending to forward it to you; but having a neighbor here who loves to laugh, I lent it to him to read; he lent it to another, and so it went the round of the Neighborhood*

On the other hand, a letter to John Adams written on June 5, 1814, gives us a different view of his reading. He wrote: *Having more leisure there [Poplar Forest] than here [Monticello] for reading I amused myself with reading seriously Plato's Republic. I am wrong however in calling it amusement, for it was the heaviest task-work I ever went through....*

Even as a boy, Jefferson had discovered that books could unlock a treasure house of knowledge and were storehouses of human wisdom. They were also life-long sources of information where he could find answers to the endless questions that fed his curious mind and elevated his spirit.

Work on Jefferson's retreat house had slowed somewhat by 1813, but during his May visit to Poplar Forest that year, Reuben Perry was finishing several inside jobs, including the installation of

The architectural elements favored by Jefferson were incorporated into the design of his octagonal retreat, including the pediment, lunette window, floor-to-ceiling windows and balustrade that mark Poplar Forest's south face.

From the Collections of Thomas Jefferson's Poplar Forest. Photograph by Jackson Smith.

the iron firebacks for the fireplaces and preparing plaster grounds for the walls.

Paramount in Jefferson's mind, however, was the new project he was eager to get underway. In other words, once again, he was ready to start "putting up and pulling down." On April 18, in a letter to John Wayles Eppes, he had briefly outlined his intentions to make an addition to the house: *The excellent dwelling house I have built there (Poplar Forest) has been associated by me with delight, and in consequence of it I have already resumed the inside finishing which I had not before intended. I have engaged a workman to build offices, have laid off a handsome curtilage connecting the house with the Tomahawk [Creek], have inclosed and divided it into suitable appendages to a Dwelling house, and have begun its improvement by planting trees of use and ornament.*

In April of 1814, Jefferson instructed his workmen to begin building a wing of offices to the east of the main house. When he used the word offices, he did not mean offices as we know them today. They were service rooms, or dependencies, used for practical purposes, such as an unheated room nearest the house, used possibly as a dairy, or storage. The largest room, twenty-four by fifteen feet, was used as the kitchen and adjoined the cook's room. The fourth room, the smokehouse, was built partially into the eastern mound.

Once again, Hugh Chisholm, Jefferson's bricklayer, did much of the work. A covered stone-paved passageway connected the wing of offices and formed the southern side of the wing. In time, Jefferson and his grandchildren enjoyed walking on the flat terrace roof that covered the wing. In one of Jefferson's letters to his daughter Martha written at Poplar Forest, he wrote: *About twilight of an evening, we sally out with the owls & bats and take our evening exercise on the terras.*

In the summer of 1814, Jefferson again wrote a letter to John Eppes, as though to convince him of the value of his retreat and perhaps express pride in his latest building enterprise: *I have this summer built a wing of offices 110 feet long, in the manner of those at Monticello, with a flat roof in the level of the floor of the house. The whole, as it now stands, could not be valued at less than 10,000 D. and I am going on....*

Once the service wing was finished and in use, Jefferson gave instructions to his workmen to begin another project. He asked them to cut wooden posts, or balusters, of heart poplar as supports for a decorative railing called a balustrade that was to encircle the roof. Though the railing was of no obvious practical value, from an architectural viewpoint, Jefferson thought rightly that a balustrade railing would add to the beauty of his villa retreat.

By 1814, the War of 1812 had grown increasingly perilous for America. The British marched inland, attacked Washington, and

Archaeologists excavated Jefferson's wing of service rooms, uncovering the original brick floor and artifacts that provided information about daily life at Poplar Forest in Jefferson's time.

From the Collections of Thomas Jefferson's Poplar Forest. Photograph by Dr. Barbara Heath.

set fire to the National Capitol building, and to what was then known as the President's House. Government officials escaped safely to Virginia.

When Jefferson received word that the British had torched the books in the Congressional Library, then housed in the Capitol, he offered his own valuable collection of books as a replacement. He thus became, indirectly, the founder of one of the world's greatest libraries. His offer to sell his entire Monticello library containing 6,487 volumes was accepted. In April 1815, Jefferson received the sum of $23,950 as payment. He used much of it to pay his most pressing debts.

A preliminary treaty to end British hostilities had been signed in Ghent in December of 1814. In February the Senate ratified the formal treaty, signed by President James Madison, ending the war. Though Jefferson had had little to do with the conflict, he shared the general feeling of relief and thankfulness across the nation after hearing the good news announcing the peace agreement.

One related episode in November of that year served as a brief reminder of the war. General Andrew Jackson of war fame, called the Hero of New Orleans by his admirers, made a surprise visit to Poplar Forest.

Jefferson supplied some of the details of the visit in a letter to his Bedford County friend, Christopher Clark:

General Jackson called on me in the forenoon, and a committee from the citizens of Lynchburg in the afternoon to invite me to partake of a dinner they give the General on Tuesday. Respect to the citizens of Lynchburg as well as the hero of N. Orleans forbade a refusal.

During his visits to Bedford County, Jefferson had acquainted himself with Lynchburg and its people. Impressed by its growth and development, on May 8, 1816, he praised the town in a letter to his friend Charles Willson Peale: *Lynchburg is perhaps the most rising place in the U.S. It is at the head of the navigation of James River and receives all the produce of the Southwestern quarter of Virginia.* In the letter he went on to mention that his "second home" was *near to Lynchburg, now the 2nd town in the state of business, and thriving with a rapidity exceeding anything we have ever seen. When I first visited that place…there was nothing but a ferry house.*

An 1816 census of Lynchburg reported that there were 3,087 individuals over the age of 16. The town limits had twice been extended, greatly increasing the acreage from the forty-five acres on which it had been established in 1786. A visitor passing through around 1816, commented that "quite decent houses for family residences are rising up with great rapidity."

A committee was appointed to take charge of the festivities in Lynchburg to honor General Jackson during his stopover on the way to Washington. The committee members also invited Thomas Jefferson, a second celebrity and a Bedford neighbor, to participate in the celebration. There was to be a public dinner at Martin's tobacco warehouse "where a most sumptous dinner was prepared and spread on tables sufficient for at least 300 seats."

The streets of the town were swept "for the occasion," and a procession of mounted cavalry escorted the two men into town. Rifle and Artillery Companies paraded on Main Street and fired "a salute."

Before all the toasts, tributes, and the "sumptous dinner" finally ended, Jefferson slipped out unobtrusively from the warehouse festivities. Though he was seventy-two years old at the time, he was anxious to return to his retreat house to prepare for an early departure the next morning on an expedition to the top of the Peaks of Otter (part of Virginia's Blue Ridge Mountains), to calculate the height of the highest peak. He arrived in good time at the home of Christopher Clark who had agreed to accompany him and several other companions on the adventure. At Clark's invitation, Jefferson, would stay at his house, located at the foot of the Peaks, until the measuring project was completed.

Equipped with surveying tools, Jefferson wanted to verify a statement he had made thirty years before in his *Notes on the State of Virginia* that *the Peaks of Otter might be higher than any others in our country, and perhaps in North America.*

At the time, in writing his *Notes* he had mentioned no specific mountain that he thought exceeded the Peaks in height, but he wanted to learn their exact height in his survey.

Soon after his arrival at Christopher Clark's house, Jefferson began to measure and re-measure the heights from *a base of 1 ¼ mile along the low grounds of the Little Otter* with *an excellent Ramsden's Theodolite of 3°1'2 radius which* he called *a mathematical apparatus.*

Jefferson continued his observations and careful calculations for five days before completing the measurements to his satisfaction. As he wrote later to a correspondent, he had found that *the height of the sharp peak above the bed of river [to be] 2,946 ½ feet, and that of the flat peak 3,103 ½ ft.* Thereafter he readily acknowledged that other mountaintops on the continent were considerably higher than those of Virginia's Blue Ridge Mountains. Among these are the peaks seen by Lewis and Clark and by another explorer, Lieutenant Zebulon Pike who discovered what is known today as Pike's Peak.

Jefferson's fascination with octagons carried over into the design of his privies—or necessaries—at his octagonal retreat, Poplar Forest.

From the Collections of Thomas Jefferson's Poplar Forest.

Photograph by Karin Sherbin.

CHAPTER 8

GRANDCHILDREN, NATURAL BRIDGE, A STATE UNIVERSITY

I promised you that I would put into the form of a bill my plan of establishing the elementary schools, without taking a cent from the literary fund. I have had leisure at this place to do this and now send you the result... The bill Jefferson proposed to be submitted to the Virginia General Assembly provided for primary, or elementary schools for all, *but also for establishing a college in every district of about eighty miles square, for the second grade of education; and for the third grade, a single university where the sciences shall be taught in their highest degree.*

> Thomas Jefferson to Joseph Cabell, a member of the General Assembly and fellow member of the Board of Visitors of what was to become the University of Virginia, in a letter written while at Poplar Forest, September 9, 1817.

In the summer of 1816, Jefferson decided that his retreat house was sufficiently finished and ready for occasional, or even frequent, visits by family members, especially grandchildren, who would make the long excursions more companionable and the stays there more pleasant.

In June, he invited two of his older granddaughters Ellen, age 20 and Cornelia Randolph, 17 at the time, to go with him to Bedford County. They were enthusiastic about the prospect and during the years to come, were to continue to accompany their grandfather far more often than any of their siblings.

The journey from Monticello to Poplar Forest usually took around three days, depending on the weather, roads, and river conditions. They traveled in a landau that Jefferson had once described as a "carriage of luxury." In 1814, he had sketched a design for a landau and directed three of his slaves to build it according to his specifications. Thereafter, for the remainder of his life, he usually traveled in his landau rather than in a two-wheeled gig or in a phaeton carriage.

John Hemings, expert carpenter and joiner, had shaped and assembled the wooden parts. Joe Fosset, a blacksmith at Monticello, had forged the ironwork, and Burwell, Jefferson's head servant, had painted the landau. Jefferson was grateful for the vehicle's relative comfort, though its somewhat odd appearance sometimes invited comments from spectators. One observer reported seeing the former president driving through Bedford County "in something resembling a mill-hopper." Another critic, Eliza House Trist, a lifelong friend, commented that she could hardly bring herself to board the landau and said that "With all due deference to Mr. Jefferson's taste, I should prefer going in any other carriage I ever rode in."

Inside the carriage, occupants faced each other on two wide seats. A convertible hood could be rolled back and forth according to the weather.

Four matching bay horses pulled the landau, which was navigated by riders astride two horses (called postilions). Israel, an experienced postilion, once described his master's landau as a "sort of double chaise" which was protected from sun and rain "by closing the covering which fall [fell] back from the middle."

Burwell, rode astride a fifth horse toward the rear of the vehicle. A cart or wagon pulled by mules carried luggage, food, and other supplies.

An odometer with a bell installed at the rear of the carriage recorded the distance traveled. Every ten miles the bell chimed, measuring the length of the journey in mileposts (markers).

The ninety-three mile trip between Albemarle and Bedford counties was undoubtedly a mixture of enjoyment and fun, boredom, potential danger, physical discomfort, and exhaustion.

In summer, travelers suffered from the heat and humidity. Dust rose in suffocating clouds from dirt-packed roads. Or, depending on the season, rain, sleet, or winter snow turned the red clay into sloughs of mud or icy drifts. Other hazards included fording streams, jerking across narrow rickety bridges, and maneuvering carriages or other wheeled vehicles around sharp curves and up and down the hilly unpaved roads of Virginia.

The route Jefferson followed most often, especially in the company of his grandchildren, led across Carter's Bridge over the Hardware River, then through southern Albemarle County to Warren, a village on the James River. Before going on, they often stayed the night at Mount Warren, the home of Jefferson's friend Wilson Cary Nicholas.

Travel the next day led through long stretches of Buckingham County countryside, with stops for meals and overnight lodging in any one of a number of taverns along the way, and in the outskirts of Buckingham Court House.

Jefferson's granddaughter Ellen had this to say about one of their overnight stops: *We always stopped at the same simple country inn, where the country-people were as much pleased to see the 'Squire,' as they always called Mr. Jefferson, as they could have been to meet their own best friends. They set out for him the best they had, gave him the nicest room, and seemed to hail his passage as an event most interesting to themselves....*

Though the travelers found overnight lodging at several regularly scheduled stops, records show that with or without grandchildren, Jefferson stayed at approximately sixteen different inns or taverns over the years.

The third day of the journey by carriage usually took the travelers to the Buckingham-Campbell County line (Appomattox County had not yet been formed), past part of Long Mountain in Rustburg, west along Candler's Mountain to Waterlick Road, and thence to Poplar Forest. The odometer registered 86.94 miles as they forded Flat Creek.

As the carriage neared the plantation, they saw an imposing house designed as an octagon with high columns at the front. The house appeared to be only one story high, but actually had two levels. The south portico overlooked a sunken lawn (or terrace) to the rear. A door under an archway beneath the portico opened into the lower floor, and to the right and left were the two necessaries, two high mounds and on the east a row of dependencies, or service rooms.

Once they arrived, Ellen and Cornelia apparently kept busy, and enjoyed their visits. Jefferson approved of "the amusements of life" and encouraged dancing for his grandchildren as a necessary social grace, and music as a source of lifelong pleasure. He also approved of drawing, which was one of Cornelia's special interests, calling the art *an innocent and engaging amusement.* Both girls also liked to do embroidery and other "fancy" work, to read and write letters, and judging from family letters to their mother at Monticello, generally entertained each other and were good companions. A favorite place for many of their activities was probably at the mahogany dining room table where light streamed in from the great skylight. Even more likely, they would have spent a good deal of time in the east bedroom where they slept in an alcove bed similar to the one in their grandfather's room. Smaller rooms, each designed to form one half of an octagon, adjoined each of the two large bedrooms. They were probably used for storage, possibly for occasional overnight guests, or other practical purposes.

New London Academy

Photograph Courtesy of New London Academy

No matter how much they enjoyed their pleasant pastimes, Ellen and Cornelia knew the importance of keeping up with their schoolwork, even when away from home. At Monticello, their mother (Jefferson's daughter Martha), taught all of her younger children, boys and girls. It is very likely that before leaving for lengthy stays at Poplar Forest, Jefferson (probably with Martha's help), drew up a list of books for their reading. Many were in French, others were ancient classics with English translations, and Ellen and Cornelia were diligent students of Latin and Greek. Their grandfather was critical of most contemporary fiction, but he may have encouraged the girls to read books of English and French literature and of course, history books, especially those written about Virginia.

Unlike the girls in the Randolph household, the older boys received advanced educations elsewhere. Jefferson took a special interest in overseeing (and paying for) the education of Francis Eppes, the only surviving child of his deceased daughter Maria.

After consulting with the boy's father, he made certain that Francis attended schools that offered the best opportunities for a superior education.

Among the schools Francis attended for a time, was New London Academy, a school located near Poplar Forest that attracted not only local boys but, as its reputation grew, young males from outside the county. During periodic visits to Poplar Forest, Jefferson became interested in the academy's teachings that apparently shared his own "vision of education." He forthwith arranged for Francis Eppes to attend the school for a time as part of his youthful education.

As early as the 1790s, the people in the vicinity of New London had become interested in establishing a "school of the first order," with a "course of instruction to embrace all branches usually taught in the best institutions." In 1795, the Virginia General Assembly approved the trustees' request for a charter and historic New London Academy (still in use today) was founded.

Officially designated a town in 1757, by order of the Bedford County court, New London is worth noting for the role it played in the Revolutionary War. An armory (later removed) was established there during the Revolution to supply cartridges and repair arms for the Continental Army. Nearby was the Oxford Iron Works, and as the population increased, stores, homes, a courthouse and other buildings gave the town an air of prosperity.

Though work on Jefferson's rural villa was far from completed by 1816, his workmen had gradually transformed what had been a framework of bricks and timber. Meanwhile, the wagonloads of furniture Jefferson had transported to Poplar Forest from Monticello, helped make the house into a pleasant, comfortable home.

Overall, Ellen and Cornelia must have approved of the house and its furnishings. As an adult, long after her visits to Poplar Forest had ended, Ellen was asked about the furniture in the house. She remarked that "*it was furnished in the simplest manner, but had a very tasty air; there was nothing common or second-rate about any part of the establishment, though there was no appearance of expense.*

New London Academy Museum

Photograph Courtesy of New London Academy

The 1816 visit was to be the first of many that Ellen and Cornelia made to Poplar Forest. In time they, like their grandfather, became acquainted with some of their Bedford County neighbors and sometimes invited them to tea or to 3 o'clock dinners.

Most of the local residents met with the girls' approval, but some did not. In one letter to her mother, Ellen described one visitor as *the very quintessence of vulgarity* but added that, *upon the whole, however, I like this place and neighborhood very much and should be well pleased to pass a part of my time here every year.*

When Jefferson made his third visit to Poplar Forest in late September 1816, his daughter Martha went along. Now mistress of Monticello, this was her first visit to her father's retreat house. On this occasion, despite the demands on her time and energy, she stayed until October. Her daughter Ellen stayed behind at Monticello as a reluctant hostess, responsible for receiving visitors and overseeing the household during her absence.

Martha and her father returned to Monticello on October 5 where she continued to carry out her countless social and household duties and care for her brood of children. Following the birth of Benjamin Franklin, the ninth in the Randolph family on July 14, 1808, she had three more children. The tenth, named Meriwether Lewis, was born January 31, 1810, and Septimia Anne, January 3, 1814. Four years later, she gave birth to George Wythe, on March, 10, 1818. Martha's first child had died in infancy, leaving a total of eleven offspring in the Randolph household.

Through the years, Jefferson continued his love affair with farming. He took delight in experimenting with new varieties of fruits and vegetables, and as his various farm and garden journals reveal, he recorded data on crop production, financial profits and losses, and other horticultural matters. Jefferson returned to Poplar Forest once again in 1816, this time in late October, with ambitious plans to beautify his landscape. In his *Planting Memoradum for Poplar Forest,* as cited in his *Garden Book,* he recorded planting *large roses of difft. kinds in the oval bed in the N. front, dwarf roses in the N.E. oval, Robinia hispida in the N.W. do, Althaeas, Gelder roses, lilacs, calycanthus, in both mounds. Privet round both Necessaries. White Jessamine along N.W. of E. offices. Azedaracs opp. 4 angles of the house.*

In a later recording in his *Garden Book* on November 22, 1816, he wrote that he had *planted 190 poplars in the grounds. 5 Athenian poplars. 2 Kentucky locusts near house. European mulberries in the new garden.*

In late November, Jefferson, with Ellen and Cornelia Randolph prepared to return to Monticello, but heavy rains descended, and what with other interruptions, still there on December 6, 1816, they received an unexpected guest whom Jefferson had previously invited to visit him at Monticello. Inadvertently, the visit had been delayed until November. Learning that Jefferson had departed for Poplar Forest, Flower made the trip to Bedford County to meet him and his granddaughters. Jefferson later identified their guest as George Flower, *the* son of an English gentleman landholder, of large family connections. To protect his privacy, Jefferson had never allowed his retreat to be overrun with visitors (as was the case at Monticello) but on this occasion, he welcomed the young Englishman warmly and their time together was apparently enjoyable.

Though the duration of his stay is not known, fortunately Flower wrote a brief description of Jefferson, his granddaughters, and the house at Poplar Forest at the time of his visit:

I found Mr. Jefferson at his Poplar Forest estate, in the western part of the State of Virginia. His house was built after the fashion of a French chateau, Octagon rooms, floors of polished oak, lofty ceilings, large mirrors betokened his French taste, acquired by his long residence in France. Mr. Jefferson's figure was rather majestic: tall (over six feet), thin, and rather high-shouldered: manners simple, kind, and courteous. His dress, in color and form, was quaint and old fashioned, plain and neat—a dark pepper-and-salt coat, cut in the old quaker fashion, with a single row of large metal buttons, knee-breeches, gray-worsted stockings, shoes fastened by large metal buckles—such was the appearance of Jefferson when I first made his acquaintance, in 1816. His two grand-daughters—Misses Randolph—well educated and accomplished young ladies, were staying with him at the time.

Despite the long journey to Poplar Forest and the return to Monticello, Jefferson continued to relish the peace and tranquility he found there, and the relative freedom from tiresome interruptions and demands on his time. He also enjoyed friendships with a number of Bedford neighbors. One was James Steptoe (Jemmy), the clerk of Bedford County Court from 1772 to 1826. His office was housed in a small building on his plantation, *Federal Hill*, a half-mile north of New London. The other close friend, Rev. Charles (Parson) Clay, lived at *Petty Grove* (later Ivy Hill) a short distance from Poplar Forest. Jefferson and Clay often visited one another to converse during his trips to Bedford and they often exchanged letters.

Jefferson wrote one particularly interesting letter to Clay, dated July 12, 1817, while sojourning at Poplar Forest. In the letter, he made a series of philosophic suggestions for wise behavior, though he did not always practice what he preached. Some of the truisms, actually written for Clay's son, are quoted below:

Never spend your money before you have it.

Never trouble another for what you can do yourself.

Never put off to tomorrow what you can do today.

Pride costs us more than hunger, thirst or cold.

Think as you please, and let others do so, so you will then have no disputes.

Take things always by the smooth handle.

When at table, remember that we never repent of having eaten or drunk too little.

As in earlier years, Jefferson continued to care little about his physical appearance, but where his grandchildren were concerned, nothing was too good, and he spared neither his time, effort, nor money in surprising them with gifts of clothing or other needs—or mere desires.

Our grandfather seemed to read our hearts, to see our invisible wishes, to be our good genius, his granddaughter Ellen once wrote, *to wave the fairy wand, to brighten our young lives by his goodness and his gifts.*

Later, in her remembrances, both at Monticello and Poplar Forest, she was also to say of her grandfather: *Such was the influence of his affectionate, cheerful temper, that his grandchildren were as much at their ease with him, as if they had not loved and honored and revered him more than any other earthly being.*

In August 1817, during a third trip to Poplar Forest since January, Jefferson decided to relax and spend more time with his granddaughters. What he had in mind was an expedition to Natural Bridge, one of the area's earliest tourist attractions, known to American and European visitors as a spectacular scenic wonder, awe-inspiring in its grandeur.

As the owner of the taxed property in Rockbridge County where the bridge was located, Jefferson felt responsible for protecting it from destruction of any kind so that future generations could enjoy its beauty. He often urged his friends to visit Natural Bridge, and he himself took excursions there during stays at Poplar Forest.

Though Ellen, Cornelia, and their grandfather began the adventure with high expectations on August 17, 1817, judging from a letter that Cornelia later wrote to her sister Virginia from Poplar Forest *it was attended with disasters and accidents from time we set off until we returned again.* She described the first day as *one of the hottest, most disagreeable days for traveling that could be.*

As they proceeded, they discovered that one of the narrow wooden spans they had to cross *was entirely gone to decay.* Bremo, the wheel horse, fell halfway through, almost dragging the carriage with him. Finally, with much shouting and pulling, they succeeded in rescuing the carriage and yanking the frightened Bremo back onto his feet. They forded the stream and went on until they came to a one-room log cabin in a clearing at the foot of the mountain occupied by an entire family who, to Cornelia's unaccustomed eyes, were shockingly uncivilized. She wrote that one of the men went about *with his hairy breast exposed,* and described another one as *the most savage looking.*

One of the uncouth mountaineers addressed the girls' grandfather as Colonel and agreed to keep the carriage safe until their return from the bridge. Jefferson had decided that he and the others with him would ride horseback across the wild, irregular Blue Ridge Mountain ridge that led to Petit's Gap.

The first night's lodging at Greenlow's Ferry proved to be a disaster. Though Cornelia later admitted to having been impressed by the exterior of the *excellent brick house as well built as the houses of Lynchburg,* she and Ellen soon discovered that the inside was a different story. The filthy rooms and the realization that they would have to spend the night in one of the bedrooms devastated both girls.

Cornelia's subsequent letter to a family member offers a detailed description of their overnight stay:

The people and the children looked as if their clothing never had been taken off since they were put on new. I felt exactly as if the place were polluted. I could not bear to touch anything, & at night. . .the sheets of our bed were dirty & we were obliged to sleep on the outside.

They set forth the following day in thick mist and when they arrived at the bridge, the skies were overcast. Fog veiled the rocks and surrounding forest. After a time, the fog lifted and the sky lightened. The black caretaker Patrick Henry, who was their guide, led them to the top of the bridge where, as Cornelia said later in the letter to her sister, they *stood on the edge & looked down with perfect safety. It is impossible to judge of the height from the top but when you go down & see how large objects are which you thought quite small you are astonished.*

Patrick Henry guided them down a steep descent for an even better view. From that point, what she had thought from the top were ferns along the creek bank turned out to be young walnut trees, and small rocks proved to be boulders. According to Cornelia's account of the magnificent scene from Cedar Creek, looking up at the bridge was *beyond anything you could possible imagine.* She agreed with the words her grandfather had written years before in his only published book *Notes on the State of Virginia* that it was t*he most sublime of nature's work.* Cornelia admitted that *she returned from the natural bridge more anxious to see it again than we were at first because it far surpassed our expectation.*

When they returned to Poplar Forest following the expedition, both girls were annoyed by the noise and dust from the construction work going on in the east wing of the house. In Ellen's August 18 letter to her mother, she described the wonders of the bridge but also mentioned the discomforts resulting from the temporary change in their sleeping quarters.

She wrote: C*ornelia and myself are not comfortably fixed. Our room has been pulled down and it will be some time before we get in it, probably a fortnight—in the meantime we are in that little close disagreeable room to the right as you enter the dining room.* She also complained about the hot weather, the crowded condition of the small bedroom, and the choking plaster dust.

On the other hand, the disgruntled girls may have exaggerated the temporary misplacement of their sleeping quarters, for

Jefferson owned the property where Natural Bridge was located and felt a great responsibility for protection of the famous geological feature.

Antique photograph courtesy of Craig Shaffer.

their grandfather wrote soon afterward to Martha at Monticello, saying that *Ellen and Cornelia are the severest students I have ever met with. They never leave their room but to come to meals . . .*

It is not definitely known what exact changes were being made to the east room, but whatever the construction or reconstruction involved, it is certain that, slave or not, John Hemings, who was a highly regarded, trusted carpenter at Poplar Forest, was one of the workmen. Jefferson knew that he could count on Hemings to do much of the finish work requiring special skills, and that other jobs, whether constructing doors, making furniture, or doing repair work, would be completed to his satisfaction. The house was painted for the first time in 1817. It was not until October 1819 that Hemings reported to Jefferson by letter that *the balustrading and the hanging of the partition doors...*had been finished.

During this particularly long stay in Bedford, Ellen and Cornelia had additional complaints to make in their letters home. In another one, again addressed to their younger sister, Virginia, Cornelia grumbled, saying that *tomorrow sister Ellen & myself have to put numbers on all of grandpapas books & it will take us nearly the whole day which I am very sorry for because besides wishing to write letters I should like very well to have copied a beautiful Desdimonia from Shakespeare which I'm afraid I cant do now.*

Cataloging the large numbers of books in their grandfather's Poplar Forest library in one day would seem to have been an almost impossible task, but knowing the importance Jefferson placed on books and reading, they undoubtedly did their best. In later years, recalling some of her memories of life at Poplar Forest, Ellen was to write that often in the evenings, her grandfather *would take his book from which he would occasionally look up to make a remark, to question us about what we were reading, or perhaps to read aloud to us from his own book, some passage which had struck him, and of which he wished to give us the benefit.*

While his granddaughters kept busy and entertained, Jefferson had much on his mind. In fact, before they returned to Monticello on September 19, he plunged into a flurry of activities that belied his usually more relaxed pace. For some years, he had been gathering ideas and plans for the establishment in Virginia of a general system of education. His idea was to begin educating children at the elementary and secondary level, in a system that would include a state university. Jefferson had long believed that no republic with a constitutional form of government could stay strong without an educated public. Over time he had made repeated attempts to stir up interest in the project in the Virginia Legislature, but had not succeeded.

In 1816, the Legislature passed a bill, drafted by Jefferson, to create Central College. Jefferson was appointed to the college's six-member Board of Visitors and began to draw up a plan. Secretly he hoped that Central, a fledgling college would become the nucleus for a state university. It would be *based on a plan so broad and liberal and modern, as to be worth patronizing with the public support, and be a temptation to the youth of other States to come and drink of the cup of knowledge and fraternize with us.*

At the first meeting of the Board of Visitors on May 5, 1817, the members had agreed to purchase two acres of land for the campus and to raise funds for the venture. After reviewing Jefferson's plans for the college, they approved the construction of the first pavilion. Each of the board members at the meeting pledged one thousand dollars.

For a time, rivalry between various Virginia towns to be selected as the site for the institution threatened to delay further action. However, in January of 1819, both houses of the General Assembly voted in favor of Charlottesville as the location. Soon thereafter, Jefferson's friend Governor Wilson Cary Nicholas wrote a letter to Jefferson from Richmond, congratulating him on his victory: *Your college is made the University of Virginia,* he wrote. *I call it yours, as you are its real founder, its commencement can only be ascribed to you. To your exertions and influence its being adopted can only be attributed.*

Jefferson already knew what kind of university he wanted. It was to be *an academical village* as he called it, with *a distinct pavilion or building for each separate professorship, these to be arranged around a square; each pavilion to contain a school-room and two apartments for the accommodation of the professor's family, and other reasonable conveniences.*

Though he consulted with and sought advice from such eminent architects as William Thornton, Benjamin Henry Latrobe and others, the credit for the general design and concept of the university rightfully belongs to Jefferson.

Jefferson's dreams for the university were lofty. He wanted an *institution where science in all its branches is taught, and in the highest degree to which the human mind has carried it.* He also wanted the architecture of the university buildings to serve as *models in architecture of the purest forms of antiquity, furnishing to the students examples of the precepts he will be taught in that art.*

The cornerstone for the first pavilion was laid on October 6, 1817. Jefferson realized that many difficulties and challenges lay ahead which would tax his mind, energies, and aging body. But there was no turning back. After seven years of retirement, he was willing to sacrifice much of his personal freedom and leisure time both at Monticello and Poplar Forest, as he renewed his *crusade against ignorance.*

Before the University of Virginia was to officially open its doors to the first students, Jefferson was destined to play many roles in its creation, both behind the scenes and openly. He involved himself in its architecture and supervised the construction. He acted as draftsman of the overall classical design of the buildings that were, in part, modeled after Palladio's drawings and concepts of architecture. He also helped hire the faculty (some of them from abroad), drafted schedules of classes, selected the subjects to be taught, outlined rules for student conduct, drew up faculty bylaws, specified requirements for examinations and for the awarding of degrees, and had a hand in initiating or supervising other miscellaneous details.

In a letter to a friend, Jefferson wrote: *The University will give employment to my remaining years and quite enough for my senile faculties. It is the last act of usefulness I can render and could I see it open I would not ask an hour more of life.*

Fortunately for Jefferson, the future of Virginia, and for the individual students from the state and the nation who would one day receive a superior education in his academical village, his wish was granted.

Jefferson's home had undergone many renovations before the nonprofit Corporation for Thomas Jefferson's Poplar Forest purchased the property. This picture shows some of the changes on the north face of the home, including a screen door, painted columns, altered stairs, and a roof without Jefferson's balustrade or Chinese railing.

From the Collections of Thomas Jefferson's Poplar Forest. Photograph by Travis McDonald.

Thomas Jefferson, a painting by Thomas Sully.

Courtesy Monticello / Thomas Jefferson Memorial Foundation, Inc..

CHAPTER 9

DEBTS, RECTOR OF A UNIVERSITY, FINAL FAREWELL

The thankfulness you express for my cares of you bespeak a feeling and good heart: but the tender recollections which bind my affection to you, are such as will for ever call for everything that I can do for you, and the comfort of my life is in the belief that you will deserve it. To my prayers that your life may be distinguished by it's worth I add the assurance of my constant & affectionate love.

Thomas Jefferson to Francis Eppes, December 17, 1821, written at Poplar Forest.

Jefferson's remark about the University of Virginia giving him employment in his old age was an understatement. The fact was that the project became the focus of his life. At the meeting of the Board of Visitors on March 29, 1819, it surprised no one that its founder was promptly elected Rector.

Meantime, despite the university's demands on his time and energy, Jefferson continued his visits to Poplar Forest. The visits were mainly for pleasure; however, sometimes he had to settle disputes within the slave community, encourage his overseer Joel Yancey to improve farming methods and crop production, or to consult with him about the livestock, which included hogs, mules, horses, sheep, milk cows and oxen.

Yancey was more dependable than many of Jefferson's former overseers, but sometimes needed his help—particularly in unexpected emergencies. One such emergency occurred during the summer of 1819. Jefferson had received a letter from Yancey in which he described a recent near-calamity caused by the greatest hailstorm he had ever seen. He then proceeded to describe the resulting damages to the house and property: *The garden is entirely destroyed,* he wrote, *and 77 panes of glass broken to atoms and the house is flooded with water. You may form some idea of destruction when I assure you that the yard was covered, and the hailstones generally larger than partridge eggs. I have been told that some were 3 inches round...I do not know what is to become of us....*

Yancey also added that it was impossible to obtain the proper-sized glass in Lynchburg to replace the broken panes. Jefferson wrote back, telling his overseer that he would bring with him *glass of one kind to repair the damages to the house, while two boxes of another kind will go up from Richmond by the first boat for Lynchburg.*

Jefferson had hoped to reach Bedford around July 7, but it was actually July 17 before he, Ellen and Cornelia arrived at Poplar Forest. The house must have looked like a disaster area. Piles of shattered window glass had left the house open to the weather. Yancey had already boarded over the skylight, leaving the once-cheerful room dark and dismal.

On closer inspection, they found other kinds of damage. Ellen wrote to her mother the following day that some of the terrace planks had been torn up by the violence of the winds, *the front of the house offering nothing but the sashes of its windows, except where they were protected by the portico.* She also complained about *floors stained by the entrance of the rainwater,* and about the musty smell in the rooms and other damage to the house and grounds. Still, she ended the letter on a more cheerful note, saying that she *felt no depression of spirits.*

To the contrary, she wrote: *there are associations and recollections, which combined with hopes for the future give me a sensation of cheerfulness and animation—I remember how profitable my former visits have been, how much more I have always carried away than I have ever brought. . .I have poured over volumes of history, which I should in vain have attempted to read at Monticello, and which were perhaps necessary to give regularity and uniformity to a shapeless mass of ideas accumulated without method or order by habits of hurried & desultory reading.*

Cornelia's tale of woe, expressed in a letter that she wrote to their sister Virginia, gives us a somewhat different interpretation of the storm and the resulting havoc: *We arrived here yesterday to dinner after one day of the hottest sun I ever felt in my life, and one of rain. . .We found that the hail storm had shattered two of grandfathers windows, in one there was not left a single pane of glass unbroken, which was the case with several of those in the other rooms, and a gust of wind since that has done nearly the same mischief to the folding doors on one side of the dining room by blowing them to suddenly. Nothing is left of the sky light but the sash.*

During that memorable summer of 1819, the threesome stayed two months at Poplar Forest. Prior to the time when John Hemings, his assistants and other workmen arrived from Monticello to make repairs, Jefferson oversaw the polishing and laying of marble on the fireplace hearths by a stonecutter named Gorman. The stonecutter so impressed his employer with his skill and dependability that Jefferson later recommended him to cut *all the stone caps, bases, sills, wall copings and newel blocks for the Rotunda, all 10 pavilions and five of the six hotels* for the university buildings under construction in Charlottesville.

During the long stay, they all suffered from the heat during some of the hottest weather on record. In August, in a letter to her sister Virginia, Ellen reported that *yesterday the temperature on the thermometer reached 99 degrees. Grandpapa thinks that such a degree of heat has never before been known in this State.* She went on to complain that *Grandpapa insisted on our using that cooler refrigerator, (I believe he calls it), which wasted our small stock of ice, and gave us butter that ran about the plate so that we could scarcely catch it, and wine about blood heat.*

On July 18, 1804, Jefferson had mentioned his purchase of a refrigerator. The machine had consisted of an oval-shaped tub set inside a tin box with holes. Ice was placed in the space between the tin & wood. In those days, ice for summer use was cut from ponds or other waterways in winter and kept in icehouses, where it could be used to combat the summer heat. There was no icehouse at Poplar Forest, however; supplies were procured from neighbors in the vicinity.

In addition to a special order of provisions from Richmond to come *by a Lynchburg boat.* Jefferson noted in his *Memorandum Book* payments for *three watermelons, six ducks, and fourteen chickens, and the purchase of other groceries during their extended stay in Bedford County.* Neighbors also added to their plantation fare with gifts of fruit of different kinds, vegetables and sometimes "sweet meats."

In early August, Jefferson had to slow his activities because of a severe bout of rheumatism that he described in a letter to Wilson Cary Nicholas as *the severest attack* he had ever experienced. *My limbs all swelled, their strength prostrate, and pain constant....*

With the help of wool flannel applied to his painful, swollen joints, along with bed rest and relaxation on his reclining "siesta" or Campeachy chair, the rheumatism attack gradually subsided. Previously, he had written to Martha about *the serious attack of that disease* and beseeched her to send by wagon one of the chairs from Monticello. These leather-covered chairs, popular at the time with a small group of Jefferson's contemporaries, were framed with a type of mahogany grown in Campeachy, Mexico. Jefferson had imported some of the chairs and instructed John Hemings to make similar copies.

Jefferson ended his August 11, 1819 letter to Martha with half-hearted optimism, saying: *we have nothing new here but comfortable rains which it is thought will make us half a crop of corn, sufficient for bread and perhaps for fattening some hogs.*

At age seventy-six, Jefferson was determined not to give in to illness of any kind. As part of his plan for good health, he continued to exercise, ate what he considered to be a healthful diet of fruits and vegetables with only moderate amounts of meat, and did not use tobacco or overly indulge in wine or beer. He had beer or cider with his meal and then three glasses of wine following dinner. He did not believe in drinking "hard" liquor like whiskey. In 1818, he told a friend, Dr. Benjamin Waterhouse, that despite his decline in body and memory, *I enjoy good health and spirits, and am as industrious a reader as when a student at college.*

In fact, Jefferson's philosophy of maintaining a sound mind in a sound body remained with him until close to the end of his life. He once listed the important qualities of a healthy mind as *good humor, integrity, industry, and science.*

Despite the summer heat, the carpenters continued with the needed repairs caused by the hailstorm. Probably the most important was the replacement of the glass in windows and, under the direction of Hemings, the re-framing of a better-designed and larger skylight over sixteen feet long and three feet wide, to replace the damaged one. Parts of the leaky shingled roof, including the deck surrounding the skylight, had to be rebuilt and the dining room ceiling re-plastered around the new construction. These and other jobs requiring skill kept the workmen occupied. In October 1819, the classically designed poplar balustrade railing finally completed by John Hemings added to the beauty of the house. He finished the blinds for the windows, hung partition doors, and completed other miscellaneous construction jobs.

Ellen and Cornelia managed to escape some of the confusion, noise, and dust created by the carpenters by visiting neighbors, accepting invitations to dinner and tea (all of which they ordinarily preferred to avoid), and at their grandfather's insistence, they entertained in return.

Letters to family members at Monticello gave reports on their visits and social life in general. Ellen confided to her mother that they sometimes mourned over the lost, wasted hours, when they accomplished nothing. Ironically, she wrote in the same August

11, 1819 letter: *This sort of life seems however to agree with us both—I have never seen Cornelia look better or handsomer.*

Cornelia was not quite so complimentary. She wrote to their sister Virginia the same day, saying that Ellen *looks better & is fatter than I ever saw her.*

On September 3, 1819, Jefferson recorded in his *Memorandum Book,* that he had paid some debts at Poplar Forest, but was barely able to cover the amount. In a brief paragraph he confessed that he had borrowed a small amount from his overseer, Joel Yancey.

Jefferson's increasing indebtedness continued to darken his future like a threatening cloud. Though he had been in debt much of his adult life, circumstances now multiplied his financial problems.

In 1819, the Bank of the United States had made a depressing announcement regarding overextended credit. Officials of the bank had decided to levy an interest charge of twelve-and-a-half percent on each dollar of all notes renewed by citizens.

Jefferson was devastated. Over the years, he had renewed his notes repeatedly because he never had enough cash money to pay them off. Though he had always tried to be optimistic and reasonably light-hearted about his debts, the new banking policy posed a dilemma that threatened his future welfare. Worse than that, it threatened his dependents and even the survival of his plantations.

He could think of only one way whereby he might be able to pay off his notes and become debt-free. The plan entailed selling off parcels of his land-holdings in Albemarle and Bedford counties.

Earlier that year, Jefferson had asked Joel Yancey, for his help in arranging the sales and promised to visit Poplar Forest in April to help with the transactions. His hopes were soon dashed. The depression of 1819, had caused the price of land to plunge and soon after arriving in Bedford, he discovered that many farmers in the surrounding countryside were almost as financially desperate as he and unable to buy more land. The same proved to be true in Albemarle. As a stopgap, he mortgaged almost everything he had—

personal and otherwise–in the hope of paying off all or most of his debts within three years.

In April of 1818, during a visit to Poplar Forest, Jefferson had created another financial problem for himself that now came back to haunt him. A notation in his *Memorandum Book* read: *Endorsed for Wilson C. Nicholas 2. notes of $10,000 D. each to the bank of the US. at Rchmnd.* At the time, Nicholas had assured him that his endorsement would not be needed longer than a year and that his promise of repayment could be relied on with "absolute certainty." Jefferson could hardly have refused the request. Nicholas was a close friend and had endorsed one of Jefferson's own notes. Another hurdle to a refusal was the fact that in 1815, his oldest grandson and namesake, Jeff Randolph, had married Jane Hollins Nicholas, the daughter of Wilson Cary Nicholas who had been governor of Virginia at the time, making him Jeff's father-in-law. After endorsing the note, Jefferson had written a short tactful letter to Nicholas, saying that as a Virginia farmer he had *no resources for meeting sudden and large calls for money.* He had ended the note more optimistically, saying that his *temporary uneasiness* would pass once there was *better management* of his farms and better growing seasons for crops.

Jefferson was comforted by continued reassurances from Nicholas that there was no reason to worry, but at the same time, he knew that his financial situation was serious. Soon afterward, he decided to deed a portion of Poplar Forest land to his grandson, Jeff Randolph, as security on the Nicholas note. Nonetheless, the loan burdened Jefferson for the rest of his life. Wilson Cary Nicholas went bankrupt sometime later, leaving Jefferson to pay $1,200 a year in interest. He could do so only by continued borrowing. Apparently the friendship between the two men survived despite the breach of trust. At his death, Nicholas was buried at Monticello.

Several reasons for Jefferson's indebtedness during his lifetime were caused by conditions beyond his control. Like any farmer, he had no choice but to accept the whims of nature–droughts, unseasonable cold, and excessive rain, diseased crops and other factors that caused low yields. Jefferson lived on credit that he could not pay back.

An additional drain on his pocketbook was entertaining the hordes of guests who continued to visit Monticello and generally, over-spending money he did not have. He also helped his daughter Martha and her husband provide for their offspring and financially assisted his widowed sister, Martha Carr, who with her six children, now lived permanently at Monticello.

Aware of her father's generosity to them all, Martha reminded him in a letter that his own needs must come first. *I can bear any thing but the idea of seeing you harassed in your old age by debts or deprived of those comforts which long habit has rendered necessary to you. The possession of millions would not compensate for one year's sadness and discomfort to you.*

Some years before, Jefferson had put his farm operations in Albemarle County in the willing and capable hands of his grandson Jeff Randolph. The young man proved to be trustworthy and hard working and it was a relief to shift some of his adult responsibilities onto younger shoulders. In 1821, he decided to give his grandson an even greater responsibility. He asked Jeff to also manage his Bedford County properties, with the agreement that in his new role he would work closely with Joel Yancey.

In a letter to Yancey written on January 4, 1821, Jefferson explained the change: *I have for sometime been becoming sensible that age was rendering me incompetent to the management of my plantations. Failure of memory, decay of attention, and a loss of energy in body and mind convince me of this; as well as the vast change for the better since my plantations have been put under the direction of my grandson T.J. Randolph. His skill, his industry and discretion satisfy me that it will be best for me to place all my plantations in Bedford as well as here, under his general care instead of my own.*

As it turned out, Yancey either misunderstood the letter, thinking Jefferson meant to replace him, or for other reasons of his own, he resigned as overseer. Jeff Randolph hired other overseers over time, and though his grandfather had asked him to manage his plantations, Jefferson continued to stay involved, especially at Poplar Forest.

Jefferson was able to take four trips to his retreat in 1821. The aging patriarch's occasional references to his ill health were justified, though he continued such activities as riding horseback into his old age. The bouts of rheumatism worsened, and over the years he had suffered from other ailments. One of these was a severe siege of skin boils in 1818; another was a brief, nearly fatal intestinal attack in 1819, that he called "obstinate colic." On the other hand, family letters bear out the fact that overall he had had remarkably good health most of his life and was still able to recover quickly from illnesses.

Jefferson's most recent recovery took place in 1822, during a springtime visit to Poplar Forest. This time, daughter Martha and various other family members accompanied him. As his granddaughter Virginia related in a letter to a family friend, her grandfather came down with *a violent cold taken in Bedford but as his sore throat has left him, and his hoarseness diminished a great deal, I trust he will soon be well.*

It rained steadily during most of their two-week visit, but apparently Jefferson recuperated quickly. Being forced by the weather to stay indoors, he had plenty of time to think about making possible architectural additions to his retreat.

On March 24, 1820, Jefferson happened not to be in Bedford when William Coffee, a sculptor and plaster worker from New York had visited Poplar Forest to consult about sculpting an ornamented entablature (or cornice) for at least one room of his retreat house. Several years passed before Jefferson was certain of the dimensions and designs he wanted, and before Coffee found time to complete the wall sculptures. During this period Coffee had also been kept busy preparing entablature ornaments for the pavilions of the University of Virginia.

Though he could ill afford any further decorative additions to his retreat house, Jefferson wrote to William Coffee, ordering decorative molded frieze ornaments for his dining room and parlor entablatures. Part of the letter read thus: *When in*

Bedford I examined the Doric entablature for which I should want ornaments he wrote. *My room will require 16 of the human busts, 20 entire, and 4 other oxsculls cut in halves and mitered for the 4 corners, to be of composition.*

Generally made with a type of plaster compound, decorative entablatures are installed inside or outside homes, or on public buildings. They have no practical use but were (and are) used to embellish. Whether added to interiors or exteriors, entablatures are divided into three parts: the cornice, the frieze, and the architrave. Jefferson used Tuscan entablatures, which are characteristically unornamented, at the north and south porticos (porches) at Poplar Forest.

The design of the interior ornaments he ordered for the dining room entablature, was of the Doric order, based on the classical "Thermae of Dioclesian." For the parlor, he requested Coffee to sculpt a frieze based on the Ionic order of the "temple of Fortuna Virilis" in Rome. The parts of the simpler Tuscan entablatures in the other rooms in the house were probably all made of wood and were unadorned. Typically, all entablatures used in interior rooms were attached to the upper part of the walls below the ceiling.

After a series of delays beyond his control Coffee wrote to Jefferson on January 3, 1823, reporting the shipment of the ornaments *to the care of Yan[cey] at Bedford House, Linchburgh,* along with instructions to John Hemings regarding their correct installation.

In 1822, Francis Eppes made a startling announcement. He told Jefferson and others in his family that he planned to marry Mary Elizabeth Cleland Randolph, who had grown up at Ashton near Monticello. The wedding was to take place November 28 at Monticello. Jefferson did not wholly approve of Francis' marriage plans—perhaps for good reason. He thought that at age twenty-one, his grandson was too young to marry, and feared that it would interrupt his education and recent efforts to "read law."

John Wayles Eppes, the young man's father, agreed with Jefferson and admitted in a letter that he did not *look forward to his {Francis'} marriage before he has completed his law reading.*

Despite all objections, preparations for the wedding went on as scheduled. The marriage took place on November 28, 1822 at Monticello.

Some years before, Jefferson had made plans to deed his retreat and at least 1000 acres of Poplar Forest land to Francis. Jefferson had given Thomas Mann Randolph and Martha land at Poplar Forest as a wedding gift and intended to give land there also to John Wayles Eppes and Maria, but had found it difficult to decide which portion to give the couple. Maria's premature death had, of course, halted the negotiations, especially when John remarried sometime later. With equality in mind, Jefferson's thinking led him to give his Poplar Forest house and at least 1000 acres of land to young Francis Eppes in place of the original wedding gift he had planned to give to his younger daughter, Maria and her husband John Wayles Eppes.

Neither the house nor Poplar Forest property would belong legally to Francis until after Jefferson's death.

However, in the meantime, Jefferson saw no reason why the young couple should not move to Bedford County at their convenience and live at Poplar Forest. Though at seventy-nine he was still able to make the three-day journey, he found it exhausting. It must have entered his mind that his trips there would become less and less frequent–and eventually have to end.

Francis and his wife Mary Elizabeth did not move to Poplar Forest until the following March in 1823. Some time before, Jefferson had fallen and broken his left arm "very near the wrist," but he still hoped to visit them in Bedford County that spring. Though his wrist and hand were still somewhat crippled from the accident, Jefferson recorded in his *Memorandum Book* that on May 14, 1823, he had set forth. Once again, his daughter Martha went along. Two of her daughters, Cornelia and Virginia, accompanied them.

Presumably, their stay was a happy one and he was undoubtedly pleased to see Francis and Elizabeth settled comfortably at his retreat. At the time, Jefferson may have anticipated repeated future visits to Bedford if his health did not worsen, but sadly, it was to be his last.

In 1824, a major event took place in Charlottesville that raised Jefferson's spirits. In August of that year, he had heard the exciting news that the Marquis de Lafayette had reached American shores in preparation for a grand tour across the United States. Welcomed as a Revolutionary War hero by most Americans, the Frenchman was greeted warmly and entertained at a series of welcoming events and festivities. One of these was a dinner in Charlottesville where he was the guest of honor.

Jefferson had not seen his old friend for over thirty-five years. After leaving France, he had hoped to return but had never taken the time to do so. Excited at the prospects of seeing his friend again, he wrote to the Marquis without delay, asking him to visit Monticello and stay as long as possible. Lafayette accepted but along the way he attended other celebrations, including one held in October at Yorktown on the anniversary of the surrender of Cornwallis that had marked the end of the Revolutionary War.

Accompanied by a military escort and a procession of admirers, the party reached Monticello in November of 1824. The reunion of the two friends began at the front portico entrance to Monticello. According to accounts, it was a touching and dramatic moment. Choking with emotion, both men cried as they embraced one another.

More high drama was to come. The next day, Jefferson attended a dinner held beneath the dome of the still-unfinished Rotunda of the University of Virginia. It was a structure of which he was particularly proud. Making use of the drawings and descriptions of Andrea Palladio, whose mid-sixteenth century architectural styles he had so long admired, he had modeled the Rotunda on a reduced scale after the Pantheon in Rome, making its diameter one half that of the Pantheon.

Jefferson had prepared a speech, praising Lafayette and thanking many of the people of Albemarle and Virginia for their friendship and loyalty through the years.

He found that his voice was too weak to read his address, but he asked a friend to read the words for him. As part of his written conclusion, he expressed with optimism his best wishes for the future success of the still unopened university and for the nation's unity and its *indissoluble union.*

Jefferson was seated between the Marquis and his longtime friend James Madison. Although the affair was a tribute to Lafayette, during the three-hour dinner Jefferson heard himself toasted repeatedly as the "founder of the University of Virginia."

On March 7, 1825, Jefferson, who had reached the age of eighty-two, had good reason to temporarily put aside his worries about debts and other concerns. It was a day for rejoicing. Quietly and without a great deal of ceremony, the University of Virginia officially opened its doors. The professor he had hired from abroad arrived in time for the event, but thus far only around thirty students had appeared on campus to attend classes at the new state institution. Others were expected to arrive on campus during the next week—once the Richmond and Fredericksburg stages were able to make their runs after weeks of cold and heavy rain.

The university buildings were finished except for some final work on the Rotunda. Despite his weakened physical condition, Jefferson was certain to have felt the deepest satisfaction and gratitude. The university he had dreamed of, fought for, and helped design and build, had become a reality. And he had been granted his wish to live long enough to see it open its doors.

At the opening ceremonies, a professor from Harvard remarked that the buildings were more beautiful than anything architectural in New England, and more appropriate to a university than can be found, perhaps in the world. Soon after the school opened, Jefferson wrote that he was *closing the last scenes of life by fashioning and fostering an establishment for the instruction of those who are to come after us. I hope its influence on their virtue, freedom, fame, and happiness, will be salutary and permanent.*

Jefferson, the positive thinker, had continued to hope through the years that profits from his farms would increase, thus enabling him to pay off at least his major debts. He hoped in vain. During the final year of his life, his unpaid accounts were more of a burden than ever. With young Jeff Randolph, who remained in charge of his land-holdings and general business affairs, Jefferson tried to devise a plan that would solve his most worrisome financial problems. Near the time of his death, Jefferson was to write James Madison about his financial ordeal: *My own debts had become considerable but not beyond the effect of some lopping of property which would have been little felt, when our friend W.C.N. gave me the coup de grace. Ever since that I have been paying 1200 D. a year interest on his debt.*

A kind of mental breakthrough occurred one night when, according to Martha, her father was *lying awake from painful thoughts."* As she said later, *Suddenly, an idea sprung into his mind like an inspiration from the realms of bliss.*

The idea was a lottery, which would require "some lopping of property," especially his holdings in Albemarle County. He now owed around $100,000. If the legislature approved the lottery venture, his grandson Jeff and other supporters could raise money by selling tickets at a fair price to bidders, then sign over pieces of property as lottery prizes.

Young Jeff saw the advantages of the plan, though his grandfather still hoped that they might save Monticello and hold onto some portions of his farmland.

As for Poplar Forest, the house and the approximately one thousand acres he had willed to Francis Eppes would not be sold. The remainder of the property would go up for sale.

After much debate, the legislature agreed to the lottery and, somewhat to Jefferson's embarrassment, advertised the sale in various regions of the nation as

Jefferson left Poplar Forest to Francis Eppes, the son of his daughter Maria. Two years after Jefferson's death, Eppes sold Poplar Forest to a local family and moved to Florida.

Florida State Photo Archives, Tallahassee, Florida.

the Jefferson Lottery. Gifts and cash benefits from friends and admirers began to arrive at Monticello from all parts of the country.

He was deeply touched. Jefferson chose to think that the gifts showed appreciation for his long years of service to his country. As it turned out, lottery tickets were printed and other preparations made, but no tickets were sold before his death.

Jefferson made his last will on March 16, 1826. Though he did not grant freedom to most of his slaves, he did free five he considered to be sufficiently experienced and skilled at their crafts to earn independent livings. However, at the time, a law existed in Virginia that required all freed slaves to leave the state and the security of their familiar plantation lives. He petitioned the legislature to grant exceptions for these slaves.

In 1826, with determined effort, Jefferson was well enough to go to the April meeting of the University's Board of Visitors and to visit his "academical village" one last time.

Sadly, a few months later, he was not able to go to Washington in June to attend the fiftieth anniversary celebration of the Declaration of Independence. In declining the invitation, he wrote that his faith in the pursuit of reason continued to sustain him in his final days and that *he counted among the blessings of self-government the free right to the unbounded exercise of reason.* It was the last letter he ever penned.

I am like an old watch, Jefferson once said of his old age, *with a pinion worn out here and a wheel there, until it can go no longer.*

Jeff Randolph said of Jefferson's final days, *His mind was always clear—it never wandered. He conversed freely, and gave directions to family members regarding his private affairs. His manner was that of a person going on a necessary journey.*

Near the end, Jefferson lapsed in and out of consciousness, but in one lucid moment, he was said to have murmured these words as a kind of benediction: *I have done for my country, and for all mankind, all that I could do; and I now resign my soul, without fear, to my God.*

Jefferson was able to hold onto life until July 4th, the fiftieth anniversary of the Declaration of Independence. He died on July 4, 1826, at fifty minutes past noon. Strange as it may seem, on that same day, his friend John Adams, once his ally for independence, also lay dying. Around noon, at his home in Quincy, Massachusetts, Adams rallied enough strength to murmur, *Thomas Jefferson survives*. However, before evening, Adams joined the great Virginian in death.

Bells rang out in Charlottesville the afternoon of July 4, in tribute to its most honored and distinguished citizen and patriot. Jefferson was buried the next day on the hillside cemetery at Monticello beside his wife Martha.

He had drawn the design and left instructions for a gravestone of coarse stone in the shape of an obelisk to mark his grave. The simple epitaph that he had written consisted only of a short list of accomplishments for which he most wanted to be remembered:

Here was buried
Thomas Jefferson
**Author of the Declaration of American Independence
of the Statute of Virginia for religious freedom
and Father of the University of Virginia.**

Through the years, the families that lived at Poplar Forest altered the home to meet changing needs and fashions. Here one can see the Greek Revival roofline constructed in the 1840s as well as some bricked-in windows on the home's southwest side.

From the Collections of Thomas Jefferson's Poplar Forest.

Suggested Further Reading About Jefferson

JUVENILE BOOKS

ANDRIST, RALPH, *To the Pacific with Lewis & Clark*. New York: American Heritage Publishing Co.,1960.

BLUMBERG, RHODA, *The Incredible Journey of Lewis and Clark. New York: Lothrop, Lee & Shepard, 1987.*

BOWERS, CLAUDE A. *The Young Jefferson (1743-1789)*. Boston, Mass: Houghton-Mifflin, 1969.

BRUNS, ROGER. *Jefferson: World Leaders Past and Present*. New York: Chelsea House Publishers, 1986

DAVIS, BURKE, *Thomas Jefferson's Virginia*. New York: Coward, McCann & Geoghegan, Inc., 1971.

FLEMING, THOMAS J., *The Man from Monticello*. New York: William Morrow & Co., 1969.

GRAFF, HENRY F., *Illustrious Americans: Thomas Jefferson*. Morristown, New Jersey: Silver Burdett Company, 1968.

JOHNSTON, JOHANNA, *Thomas Jefferson His Many Talents*. New York: Dodd Meade & CO., 1961.

MELTZER, MILTON, *Thomas Jefferson (The Revolutionary Aristocrat)*. New York: Franklin Watts, Inc., 1995.

PATTERSON, CHARLES, *Thomas Jefferson*. New York: Franklin Watts, 1907.

WIBBERELY, LEONARD, *Time of the Harvest (1801-1826)*, one of a series on Jefferson (Ariel Books). New York: Farrar, Straus & Giroux, 1966.

ADULT BOOKS

AMBROSE, STEPHEN E. *Undaunted Courage. Meriwether Lewis, Thomas Jefferson, And The Opening of the American West.* New York: Simon & Schuster, 1997.

BETTS, EDWIN MORRIS & BEAR, JAMES ADAM, JR. *The Family Letters of Thomas Jefferson.* Charlottesville, Virginia: University Press of Virginia, 1986.

CHAMBERS, S. ALLEN, JR. *Poplar Forest and Thomas Jefferson.* Published for the Corporation of Jefferson's Poplar Forest in commemoration of the 250th anniversary of the birth of Thomas Jefferson, 1993.

CUNNINGHAM, NOBLE E. *The Life of Thomas Jefferson: In Pursuit of Reason.* New York: Ballantine Books, 1987.

HEATH, BARBARA J. *Hidden Lives The Archaeology of Slave Life at Thomas Jefferson's Poplar Forest.* University Press of Virginia, Charlottesville and London, 1999.

HOLMES, JOHN M. *Thomas Jefferson Treats Himself (Herbs, Physicke, and Nutrition in Early America).* Fort Valley, Virginia: Loft Press. 1997.

HORN, JOAN L. *Thomas Jefferson's Poplar Forest, A Private Place. Corporation for Thomas Jefferson's Poplar Forest, 2002.*

JEFFERSON, THOMAS. *Notes on the State of Virginia.* Edited by William Peden. New York: W.W. Norton & Company Inc.: London: W.W. Norton & Company, Ltd., 1982.

KOCH, ADRIENNE & PEDEN, WILLIAM. *The Life and Selected Writings of Thomas Jefferson.* Edited, and with an Introduction. New York: Random House (The Modern Library Division), 1944.

LANGHORNE, ELIZABETH. *Monticello a Family Story.* Chapel Hill, North Carolina: Algonquin Books, 1987.

LLEWELLYN, ROBERT. *Mr. Jefferson's Upland Virginia. A Photographic Celebration of Thomas Jefferson's Homeland.* Charlottesville, Virginia: Upland Publishing, Inc., 1979, Second Printing by Thomasson-Grant, Inc., Charlottesville, Virginia, 1983.

MALONE, DUMAS. *The Sage of Monticello.* One of six volumes in Malone's series *Jefferson and His Time,* 1981. Boston: Little Brown and Company, 1981.

MALONE, DUMAS. *Jefferson the Virginian.* Ibid.

MAYO, BERNARD. *Jefferson Himself. The Personal Narrative of a Many-Sided American.* Edited by Bernard Mayo. Charlottesville, Virginia: The University Press of Virginia, reprinted by arrangement with Houghton Mifflin Company and Bernard Mayo, 1970. Sixth Printing 1984.

MCLAUGHLIN, JACK. *Jefferson and Monticello. The Biography of a Builder.* New York: Henry Holt and Company, 1990

The Story of New London Academy 1795-1945. Published by Order of the Board of Managers of New London Academy. Forest, Virginia, February 1945.

ARTICLES

BEEBE, LYNN A. "Going on to Achieve Jefferson's Vision." *Thomas Jefferson's Poplar Forest Annual Report. 1997.*

BROWN, C. ALLAN. "Thomas Jefferson's Poplar Forest: the mathematics of an ideal villa." An article in published form reprinted from *The Journal of Garden History.* Vol. *10,* no. 2, 117-139, 1990.

HARRIS, MARTHA TERRELL. "Thomas Jefferson's Escape to Geddes Farm in Amherst County." *Lynch's Ferry, A Journal of Local History.* Lynchburg, Virginia: Warwick House Publishing, Vol. 1, no. 1: 28-30, Fall issue, 1988.

HEATH, BARBARA. "Discovering the Plantation World of Poplar Forest." Included in a collection of articles by staff members of Poplar Forest. In *Notes on the State of Poplar Forest*. Volume 11, 13-19. 1994. Published by: The Corporation for Thomas Jefferson's Poplar Forest.

MCDONALD, TRAVIS C., JR. "Restoring Jefferson's House: Grand Design Emerges." In *Poplar Forest Annual Report 10-12. 1996.*

MCDONALD, TRAVIS C., JR. "Poplar Forest: Synthesis of a Lifetime." Lead article in a collection of articles by staff members of Poplar Forest. In *Notes on the State of Poplar Forest*. Volume 11. 1-7, 1944. Published by The Corporation for Thomas Jefferson's Poplar Forest.

SHAFFER, JANET. "New London." Article in *Virginia Cavalcade*, winter 1966 issue, Richmond, Va. A reprint of the article was also published in *Lynchburg Magazine,* November, 1969 issue.

WATSON, LUCILLE MCWANE. "Thomas Jefferson's Other Home." *The Magazine Antiques 71 342-46, April 1957.*

Additional references include a wide assortment of excerpts from magazines, journals, and other publications which have been provided by the Interpretation staff as "required" reading for volunteers who conduct tours and otherwise help to educate the visiting public about Jefferson's Poplar Forest house and grounds. Another valuable source has been S. Allen Chambers' excellent volume entitled "Poplar Forest and Thomas Jefferson" as noted in the Preface, Acknowledgements and Bibliography. Readers with an interest in tracing the early history of the plantation that pre-dates Jefferson's retreat house, can find this information in Chambers' volume, Chapter 1, pages 1-5.

Quotes by Thomas Jefferson

I am happier while reading the history of ancient men than of modern times.

To William Duane, 1813

Give about two hours every day to exercise; for health must not be sacrificed to learning. A strong body makes the mind strong.

To Peter Carr, 1785

My God! How little do my countrymen know what gracious blessings they are in possession of, and which no other people on earth enjoy.

To James Monroe, 1785

I am an enthusiast on the subject of the arts, but it is an enthusiasm of which I am not ashamed, as its object is to improve the taste of my countrymen, to increase their reputation, to reconcile to them the respect of the world, and procure them its praise.

To James Madison, 1785

I know of no safe depository of the ultimate powers of the society but the people themselves; and if we think them not enlightened enough to exercise their control with a wholesome discretion, the remedy is not to take it from them, but to inform their discretion by education. This is the true corrective of abuses of constitutional power.

To William C. Jarvis, 1820

If a nation expects to be ignorant and free, in a state of civilization, it expects what never was and never will be.

To Charles Yancey, 1816

Educate and inform the whole mass of the people. Enable them to see that it is their interest to preserve peace and order & they will preserve them.

To Dr. Richard Price, 1789

About the Author

In 1984, fascinated with the exciting plans to restore Thomas Jefferson's 1806 retreat house and grounds to their original magnificence, Janet Shaffer signed on as a volunteer docent to interpret the Bedford County plantation to the first interested visitors. She is still there and still learning as the leaders of the Corporation for Thomas Jefferson's Poplar Forest initiate and oversee the intensive research process that precedes each phase in the step-by-step process of restoring a historically significant national treasure.

This abbreviated biography of Jefferson and the story of his retreat house is the author's second published book to focus on history. The first was *Peter Francisco—Virginia Giant,* a fact-fiction book about the extraordinary exploits of an American hero during the Revolutionary War. At present, she is completing a novel, working on a book of essays and occasionally conducts writer's workshops and seminars.

A writer for over thirty-five years, Janet Shaffer's short fiction and non-fiction articles have been published in a wide variety of state and national periodicals and journals. Hundreds of her features and news stories appeared in newspapers during her twelve years as writer and media contact in public relations at Randolph-Macon Woman's College.

She has three grown children and lives with her husband in a historic house bordering Jefferson's original Poplar Forest tract of over 4,800 acres. A prize-winning artist and photographer, she stays busy writing and painting, and among other diversions, keeping in touch with her eclectic circle of friends.

689058

Made in the USA